AF362002

a universe humanised

nero suno

First published in 2019

Copyright © Nero Suno 2019

The right of Nero Suno
to be identified as the creator of this work
has been asserted in accordance with
the Copyright, Designs and Patents Act of 1988.

All Rights Reserved.
No part of this publication may be reproduced,
stored in a retrieval system,
or transmitted in any form or by any means,
electronic, mechanical, photocopying, recording,
or otherwise,
without the prior permission of
the copyright owner.

Poetry and Art by Nero Suno
Book design by Nero Suno

ISBN 978-3-9821099-1-6

www.nerosuno.com

CONTENTS

There

Here

Here

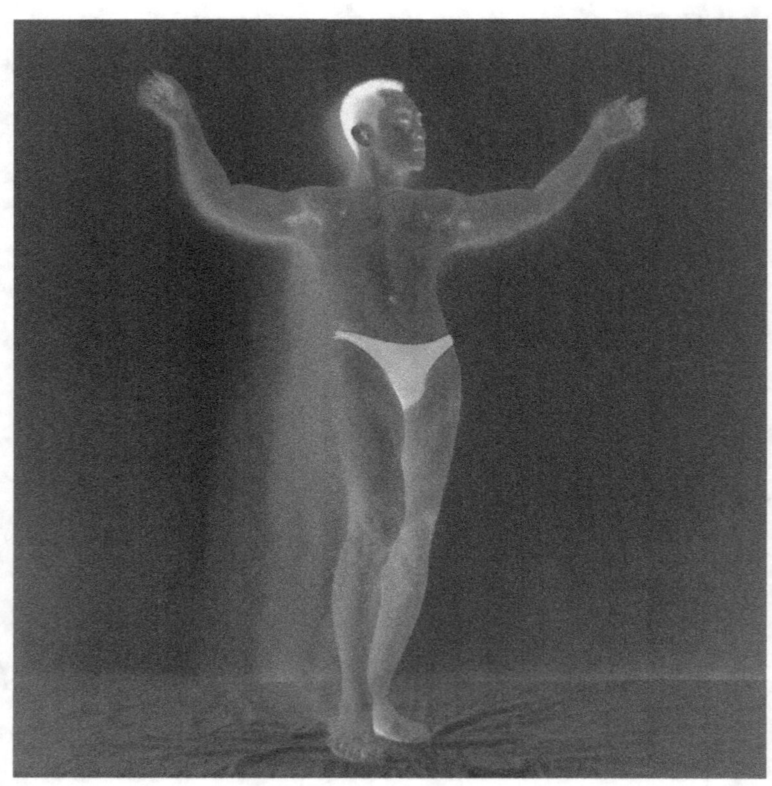

Here

Here is where life is full of me.
I spin in the absolute now,
killing every possible no.
I rejoice: life is fully mine!

All my needs and wants answer "yes";
all my dreams become generous.
I praise the long struggling years,
each moment engraved on my face.

Let me kiss the haters nearby
and the future lovers beyond.
Both my body and soul, I bare;
no emotion feels left behind.

Still, the world is a joke to mock;
I mock myself being a joke.
Wish my life enjoy like a fuck
with the bliss in a touch of luck.

Eternity is my age

Eternity is my age

Eternity is my age

Eternity is my age;
my body is infinity.
I am all that is out there to be;
I have all that is out there to have.

The wind is the bird flying in it;
the sea is the fish swimming in it.
I am both a bird and a fish inside;
I have a world where winds fly and seas swim.

Infinity is my age,
my body is eternity.
I am all that is out there to be;
I have all that is out there to have.

I'll live this moment

I'll live this moment without fearing death,
should death arrive in time, nevertheless.
Should love arrive before all surprises,
let the true bliss guide me to paradise.

Now I spiritualise my body,
it breathes, moves and grows universally.

I'll live without thinking or thoughts for once.
I'll learn to feel with my whole existence.
Miracles start to understand themselves;
mysteries are nature being itself.

Now I corporealise my spirit,
it brings life back to life eternally.

Having is

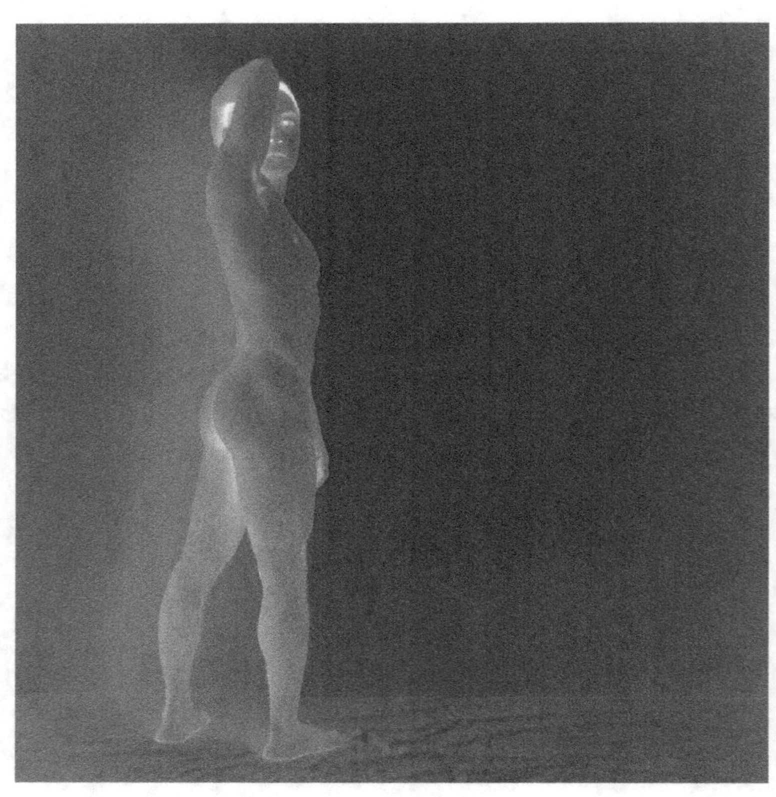

Having is

Having is
          simultaneously
losing
     when keeping keeps being nothing.

I am had,
          simultaneously
the whole world is lost in me;
                         half the world
keeps becoming the whole of everything
(that was and will be nothing in no time).

And no time has something to lose for me,
with time itself keeping
                    being
                         nothing.

How many times

How many times

How many times could time survive
all things on earth except the end?
More than the times of beginnings
in the middle of everywhere.

Life and death transform into death and life
naturally and humanly, constantly.
War and peace misunderstand peace and war
permanantly or temporarily.

So many times time has survived
at least by not trying again.
The ends conceive the beginnings
in the middle of everywhen.

Present misses being futuristic
until it sees itself in history.
Until it sees history in itself,
future misses being present only.

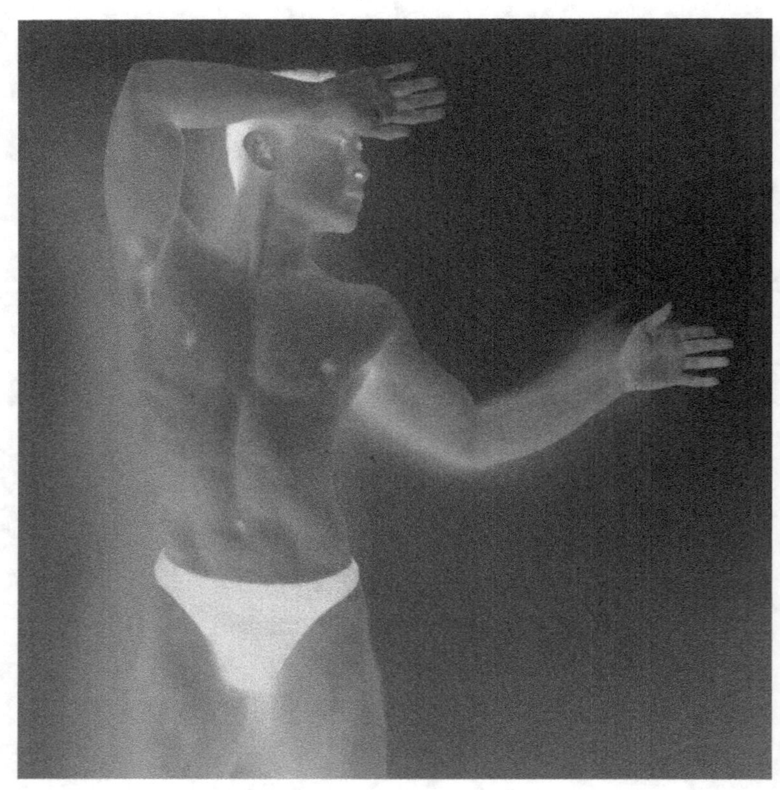

now i feel Spring

now i feel Spring before nothing
false wants to immediate my feelings

and i selfish whose feelings of Spring
greening the world (belongs to happy all
because yes Spring answers me knowing why
love is first and foremost feel) if it is

my whole life envies every last year re
turning differently same another
summer (always rains enough then leaves of
autumn inspire winter better farewells)

poetry (lost to find imagined love)
composes itself as Spring does myself

Word by word

13

Word by word

Word by word, imagination explores
all the unimaginable joy
bluming open&closely in my mind
as my body turns into every flower
bluming close&openly by itself.

Sun&moon permitting, a word
kisses its syntax whose heart beats
with the tongue in my mouth.

And poetry should imagine that
colors are content of the fifth season;
silence&sounds understand each other.

Word by word, I turn into a garden
among a sea of wonderments
where god is something to believe in.

Bring me flowers

Bring me flowers if the strong arms of yours
could bear the lightness of my love.

                                                         My love
flourishes only in beauty and joy.

Yes, my love needs beauty and joy only.

Let the world carry its own heaviness,
since as long as time, history has failed
to tell someone's story where ugliness
and pain fool a fool better than themselves.

Among all that survive either birth or
death, living perfectly in beauty and
joy, flowers are born to die in their youth.

In my youth, my love must be loved by you
whose love is received from trees and grass.

                                                                 Wait
until every seed turns into flowers.

Till Spring ends

Till Spring ends, my dry spell is your dry spell.

Yet do we feel patiently seasonal
when seasons are changeful as we are?

If Winter grants Summer's ardor to rain,
yes, but if the sun forbids enough snow,
no, since Autumn still casts the best spell.

Till Autumn spends an entire year on us,
Spring anticipates the end of itself,
before both Summer and Winter should grudge
each other's opposite eternally.

Dear autumn

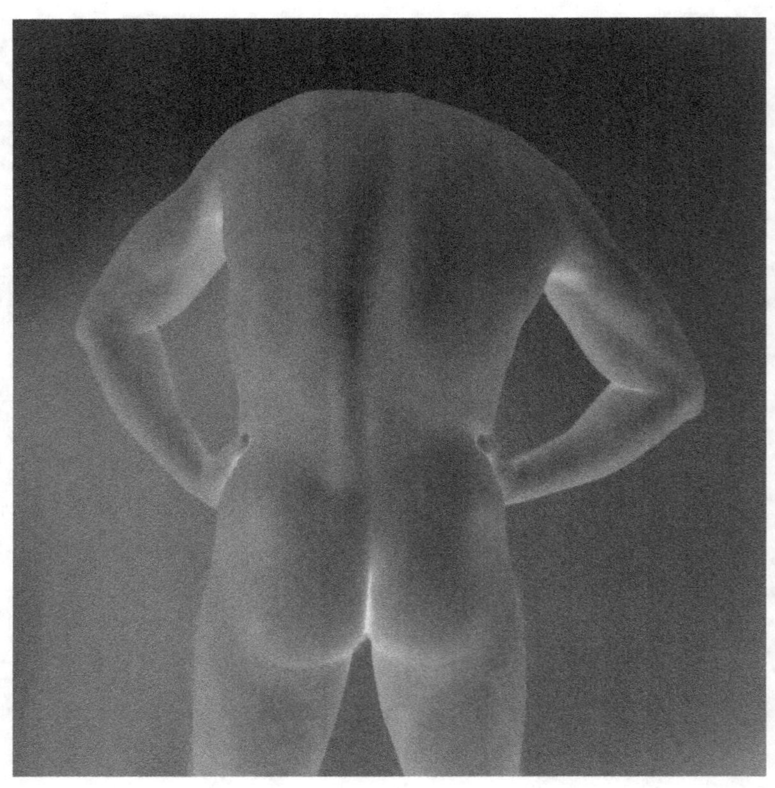

Dear autumn

Dear autumn,

I beg you for some gold
(just enough for me to
recall how sorrow could
obscure anything as
colorful as you are
more fateful than changeful),

if not the entire world.

What if

I want the entire world
(too much of nothing makes
too few of all mistakes
that force me to give up
my life already gone),

before

you leave me for the cold?

My family

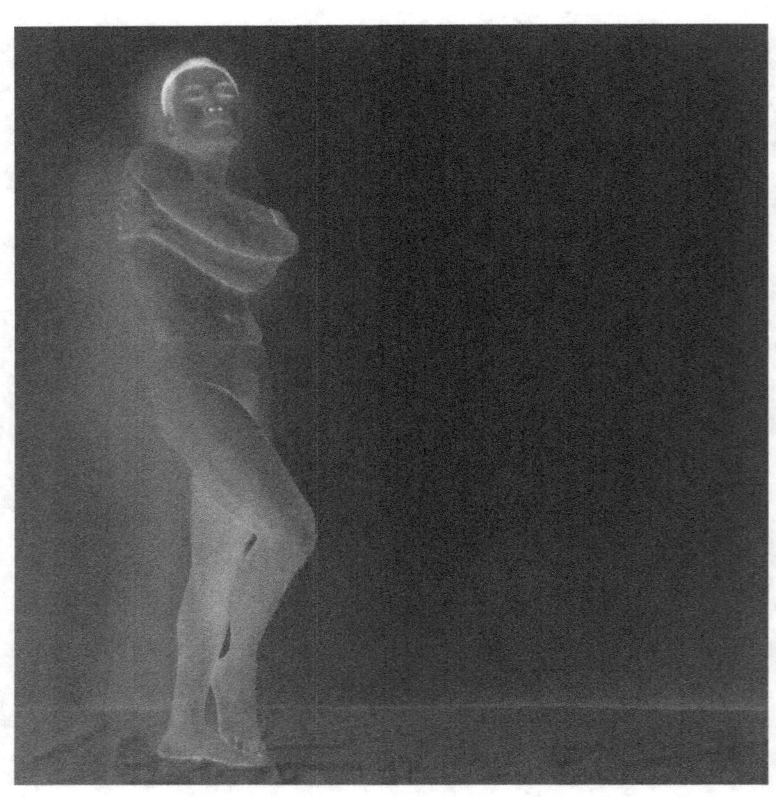

My family

I am a man with no country,
but I am a branch of my family.
I am (un)happy for this coincidence
(my destiny on it depends).

I go wonder where I will be,
then I wander back to my family
who remember my (un)forgotten childhood
(I stay a child still, as I should).

I often look for a meaning,
and I find answers in my family:
It is because love is (un)conditional
(on condition that love is all).

My father

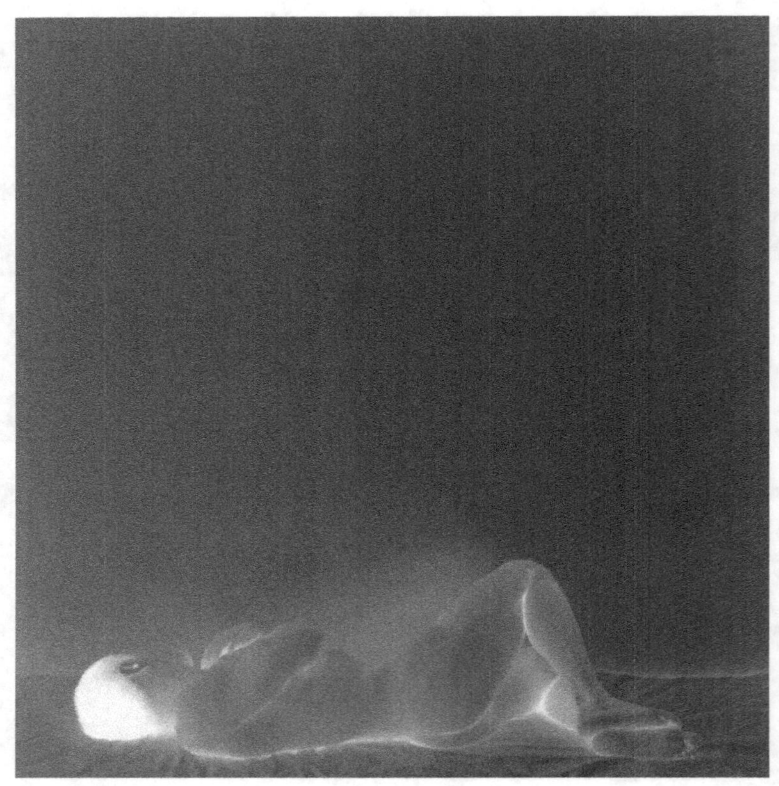

My father

My father and I love each other now he died
because why I loved him not enough while he lived
he was a father normal he tried best he could
I was a son abnormal I made him not proud

My father became my father at my age young
he thought days never grow old years never hide
until winters kept promises summers changed vows
and he understood things that I will never not

My father had dreams so small inside hopes so big
but destiny is jealous of all happiness
still he moved on with the weight of a family
in a heartbeat, he substitued youth for duty

My father drank much sometimes he had thirst for life
sometimes he was enraged feeling weak like a child
sometimes he looked at me and cried and cried and cried
for the very last time I was his second chance

My father would often remember his father
disclosing regrets of love taken not given
as a son too he should not blame me for my wrong
as a son too he should know how much I miss him

25

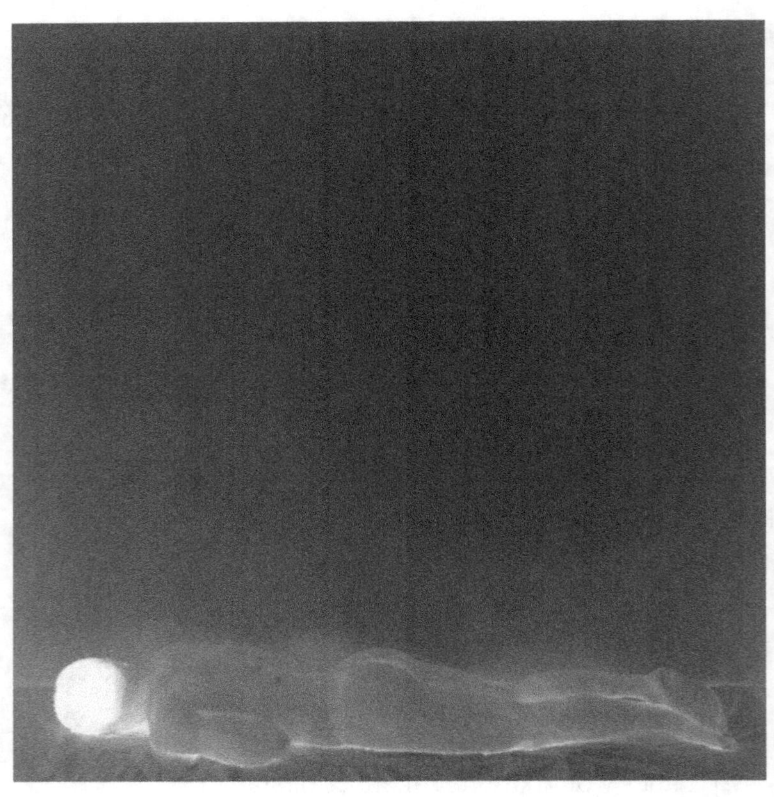

My mother

My mother

26

My mother is mothers of all sons
of whom I am each and every one.

My twin

My twin

My twin,
he is as universal as
I am as personal as
he is as neutral as
I am as extreme as
he is as spiritual as
I am as physical as
he is as common as
I am as special as
he is as distant as
I am as close as
he is as human as
I am as animal as
he is as feminin as
I am as masculin as
he is as real as
I am lacking of myself as
my twin.

My solitude

My solitude

My solitude exceeds one hundred years
(long enough for anyone to survive).
Now I am in my hundredth year (with tears
more wet than dry), more asleep than alive.

I loved life either much or not at all.
Against the whole world, what else could I do?
I loved myself (flying too high to fall)
like no other selves (who loved themselves, too).

Memories are the last ever to last
until I forget how to be a child.
Years, (the rest of) which I miss still move fast
though I (try to) remember how to smile.

Love is

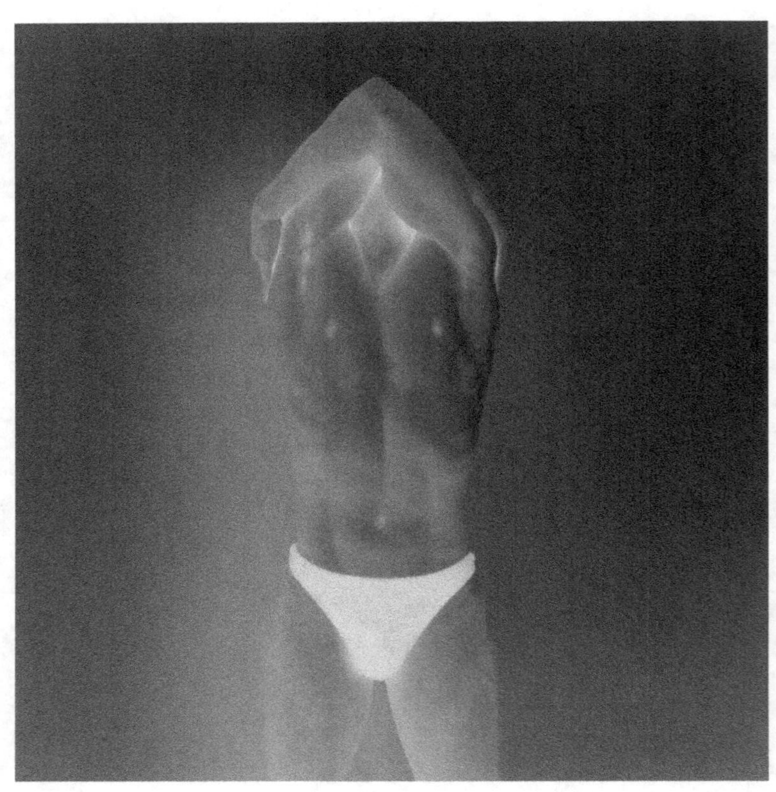

Love is

31

Love is

32

Love is no more the biggest challenge
in the face of life and death (all fail
except time whose meaning is to change)
but the smallest wonder for the few.

Love is always the biggest prison,
the prisoners not craving freedom.

Love is, by far, the biggest circle.

My body understands love

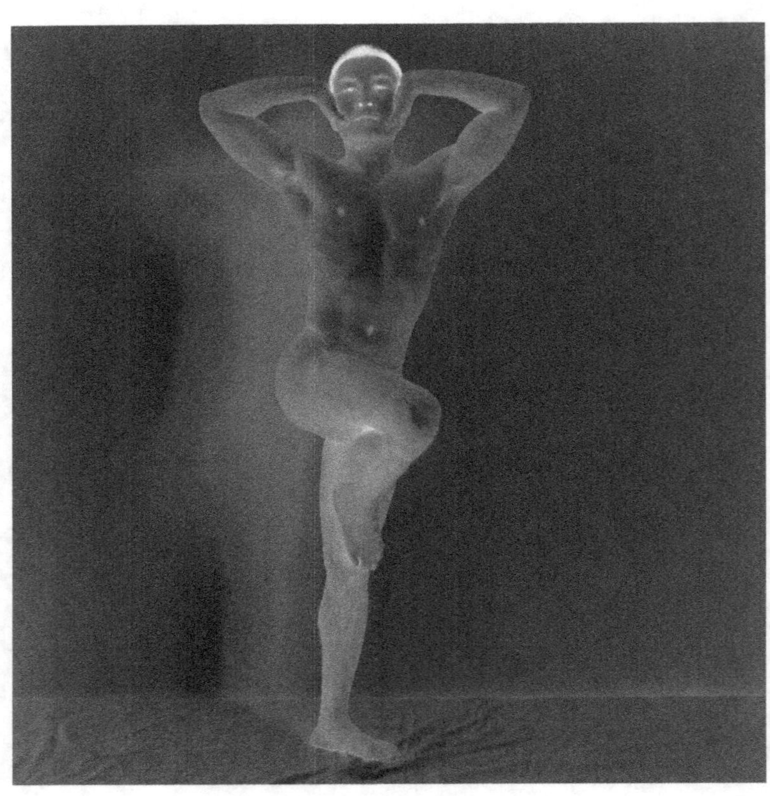

My body understands love

34

My body understands love before
my soul misunderstands sex.

                        Love is
everything more understandable
than itself to live for, if sex is
nothing misunderstood to die for.

I desire a body as much as
a soul spiritualises love.

Love realises sex above all.

Love is sooner far

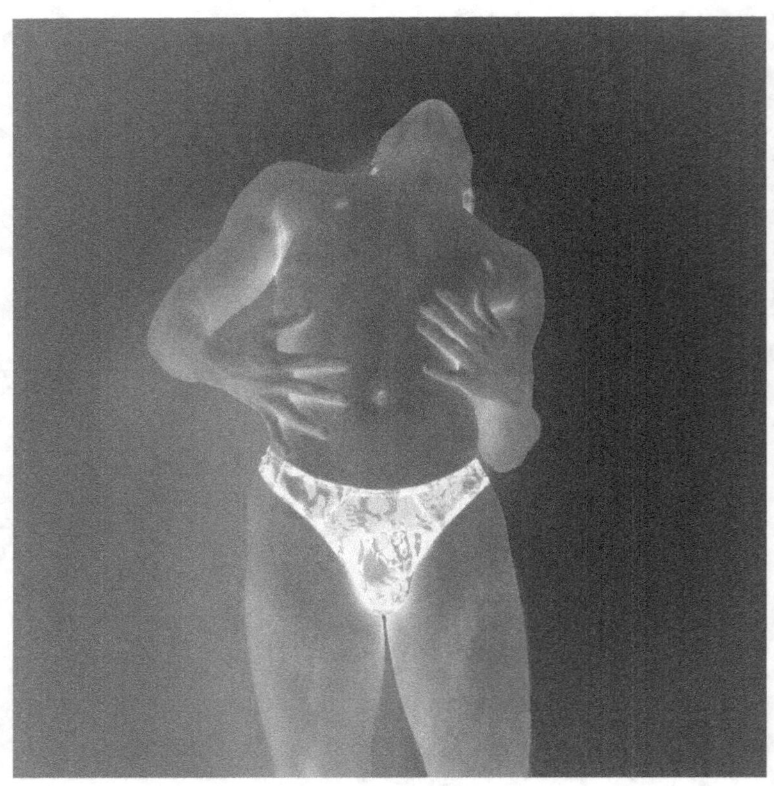

Love is sooner far

Love is sooner far than later near, and
never wherever we are together
(whenever we are together, love is
as near as nowhere).

                        Love is as far as
somewhere unknown in a heart forever.

I am more you than you are less me, and
either of us need what both of us want
(what needed is enough to be wanted)
until life takes everything that it gives.

I give everything that you do not take.

enough love

enough love should not satisfy Eros
among mortals.
                    enough love should not do.

enough love should ever outgrow itself
into now when here is the truest yes.
and no raises immortally Pysche
by the most beauty attached on her wings.

enough love should fall deep down with beauty
as Eros and Pysche fly high above
beyond mythologies.

                    realities
realise us with sexuality,
because in real dreams, nothing is enough
if enough of everything is dreamed of.

Love must do what it has to be

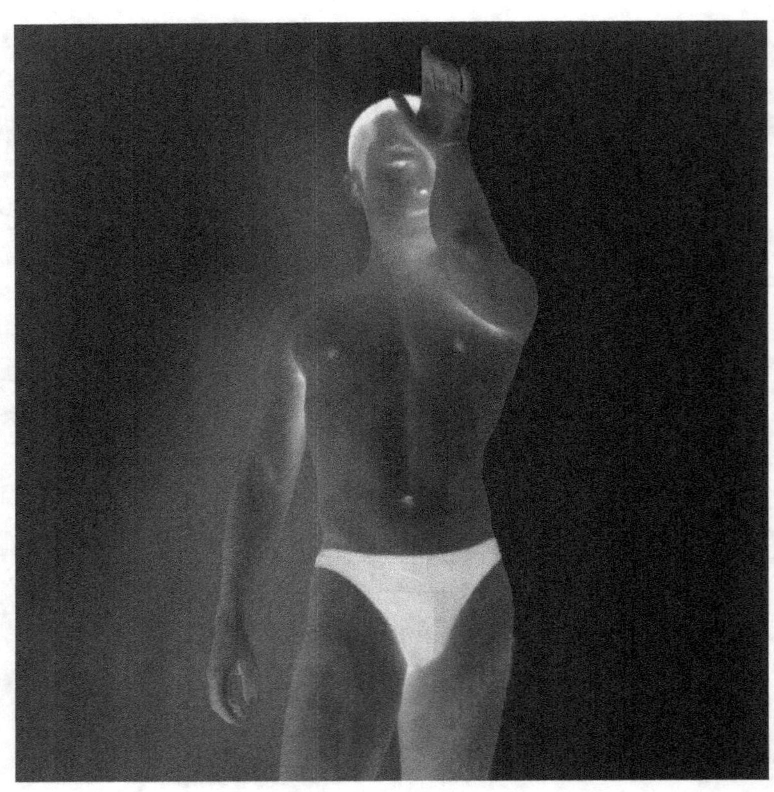

Love must do what it has to be

Love must do what it has to be maybe
where follows hate doing how indeed,
still, which one fails to try the one who feels
a heart breaks, bleeds and why or why not heals?

This was that now sooner all are the same,
but only the self hears the whole world cry.
Nothing real is more unreal than a dream,
thus everything stays dreamy till love dies.

Love must be what it has to do firstly
when precedes hate being how lastly,
still, which one pretends seems the one who wins
a heart to lose and why or why not find?

I was you now later we are the same,
for both egos disillusion both souls.
Let your saddest saddness remember me;
let our happiest happiness make love.

Your beauty

Your beauty
           kills
                   my unwilling to love,
I am hereby more than sexually
grateful to you.

Your beauty saves my willing to be loved
which saves me from all loveless living things,
I am
        hereby
                more than
                            sexually
heroic and most innocent.

I am ready to save this ugly world.

Your beauty is my beauty,
our sex is hereby more than sexually
perfect in this beautiful world.

I lust for you

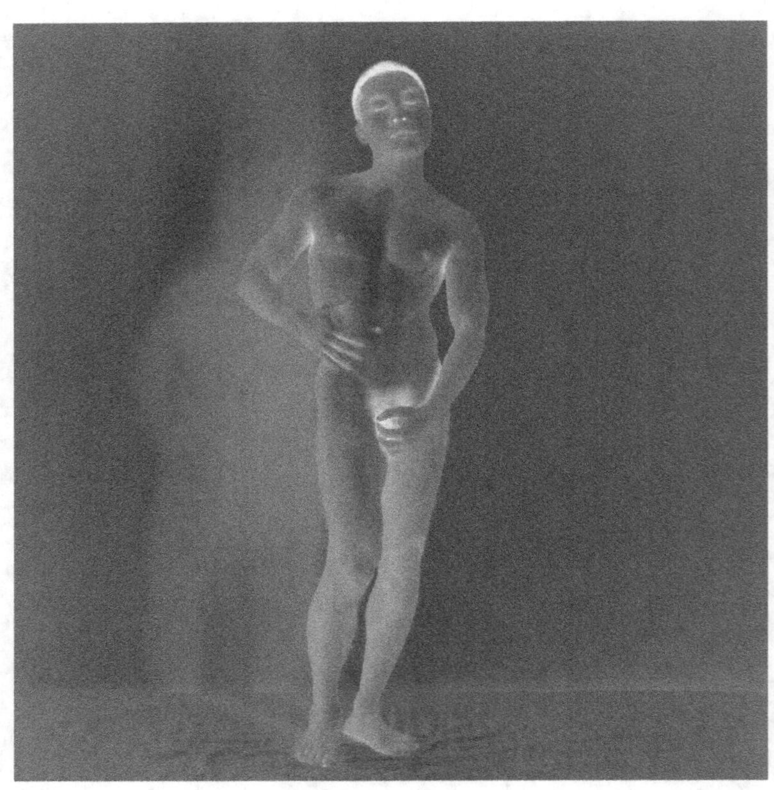

I lust for you

I lust for you with my absolute desire
&
I'm optimised by such confidence
that it'll not fade away too soon at all,
for my absolute lust for you
is soyetbecause stronger than
why&how you're
powerfully beautiful,
beautifully seductive,
seductively desirable.

I lust for you with my possible love
that'll indeed strengthen,
a phenomenon
that I'm (body&soul)ly unprepared to explore
but with you(r beauty)
for the last(first)ly first(last) time
&
my life,
henceforward,
will begin&end with you.

Owning you wholly

45

Owning you wholly

Owning you wholly is how I love you
entirely.

        I must own your thinking
(such will be my will lastly) until
you think of me firstly and only
no matter wherewhen you are with
or without me.

            I must own your time
remembering me in your past
and your present is already mine
(your future stays with me forever).

I must own your body.
                O your body
feels better than to know
(all seasons of Spring, all months in May)
my body which knows how to feel.

My owning you is your owning me.

In imagined intercourse

In imagined intercourse, our motions
flow around our emotions at their peak
as my masculinity grows younger
than your feminality in its prime.

Only imagination itself knows
how it should feel when we do what we do
(each becoming the other inside out;
the other becoming both outside in).

Now we are wherever we need to be
(before and after time never runs out),
until time is not any longer short.

Could all this strangeness be so familiar
as every strange wish which could not happen?
Yes but no, if (n)either one of us love.

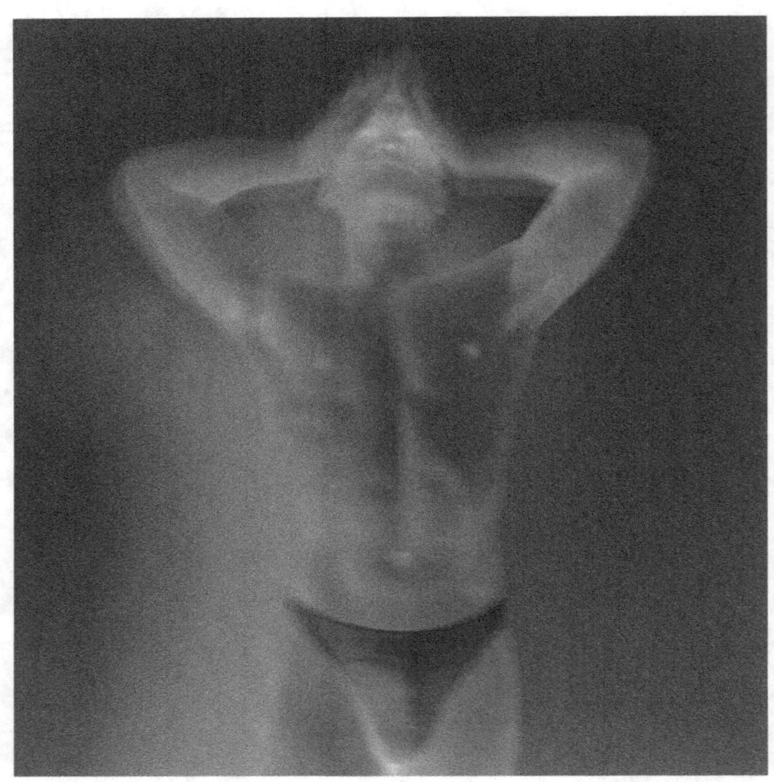

Mein Schatz, I kiss you

Mein Schatz, I kiss you
(with my mind thinking
of you kissing me with your mind thinking
nothing else
but to kiss me)
in this moment when
the world seems no more a lie to believe
as
a kiss seems the only truth.

I am a poet

I am a poet and you are my last poem
after which I shall no longer have words
but to touch and touch, feel and kiss
you until all my poems have become.

I see my own eyes with the world whose
each color finds a flower, each sound
hears music in each happening now
(you touch and touch, feel and kiss me).

More by early more, I am melting
into the poem, swimmingly enough,
which you are made of, a most beauty.

And eventually we are everything
that is touching, feeling and kissing
(a natural miracle needing time only).

53

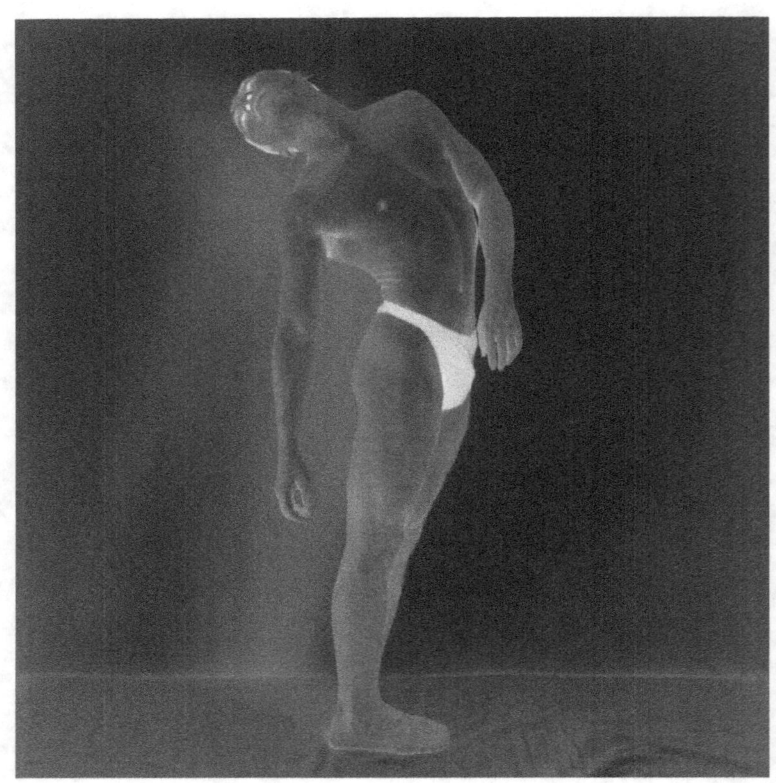

Whoever opens my heart

54

whoever opens my heart
will keep it open forever.
he must be magical
for my heart is a lock without a key.
(my heart is a lock locked by love,
my body a prison prisoned by desire.)
only magic may break to make
my new life that is open and free.
my new life would be
how a life should be.

love and desire will become me;
i shall become as magical as he.

How do I wish to know

How do I wish to know

How do I wish to know that I wishfully
love you?

        By imagining the most
imagined power, love. Love being love,
it craves sex, the forever sensation,
from the time when the world seems enough.

My body of extreme poverty is dying
to be reborn in full richness inside
your body of supreme beauty, and
as one, we feel seasons of spring now.

Love is virgin when sex grows young
like the fingers of trees in spring, touching
lovers of us who are lovers of all.

57

Someday when you'll be someone's

Someday when you'll be someone's,
don't dive into your happiness yet,
for much happiness you let,
I'll be drowning
in my love for you,
and in my pain, sinking.

Someday when someone claims
your body of beauty,
he'll be the king of luck
favoured by this
                    more hateful than hateable
                                        life.

May you be his forever queen,
or
I'll punish fate for being jealous of my dream.
I'll punish time for being jealous of my queen,
should
you fail to be his forever dream.

I lay me down

59

I lay me down

I lay me down

I lay me down to think of you
intensively (with my most strength)
in my bed (where you never were)
where nights feel colder than my grave.

And I need not certainly die
(if life be a choice, not a must)
to give up (not to give you up,
but to take or make enough grief).

How I miss you physically
at least (for spiritually,
your beauty falls beyond this world)
at this hour growing into death...

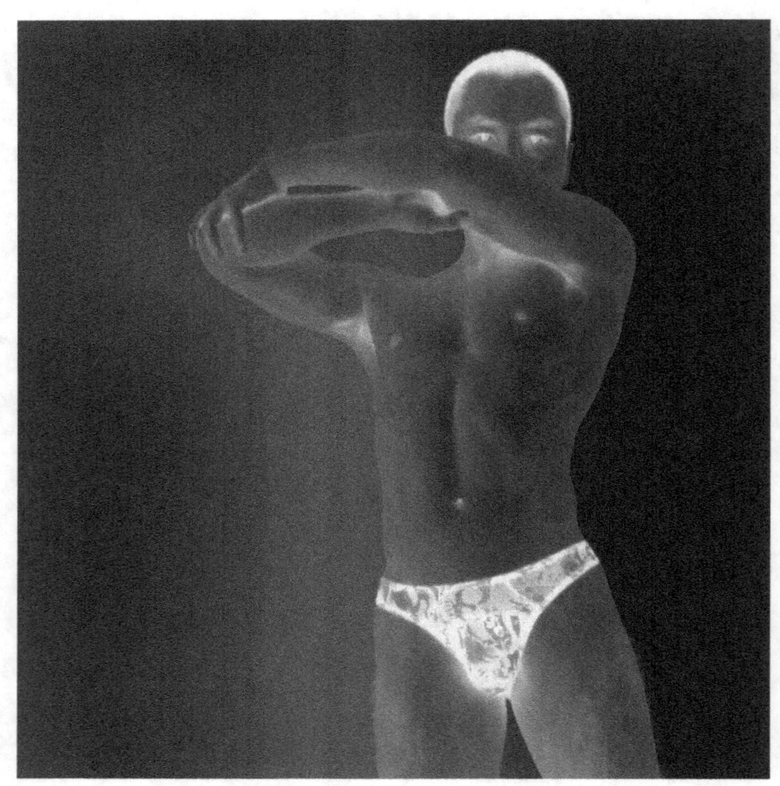

Help a man

Help a man grow back into a child,
hence
his world should again
seem real in dreams.

I am a man dreaming in a child,
but
why does not my world
seem real as it should be?

Either the world is or I am
an unreal dream.

The fact is a miracle

The fact is a miracle

The fact that no miracle has happened to me
is matter-of-factly
a factual miracle
(among all miraculous facts)
that is miraculously happening to
the fact that no miracle has happend to me.

The fact is a miracle
that is happening to the fact.

The fact is a miracle.

A liar named

A liar named possibility breaks
more than any impossible lie makes,
with all the same difference uniting
as one:
          the absolute truth that denies.

But all the different sameness divides
subjects into objects and vise versa.

Thus,
        a nameless liar must pick a side
among yes,
                no,
                    the truth,
                              et cetera.

Cause & Consequence

Life is the cause of all consequences
causing new causes, such as war & peace
among other human experiences
that consequently cause the universe

to dehumanise Heaven in Hell
called planet earth where humans live to kill
no more than animals kill to live, till
trees feel the pain of growing miracles.

Life is the consequence of all causes
ending old consequences, such as love
above certain human disenchantments
that make planet earth go around, of course.

Killing sentences the meaning

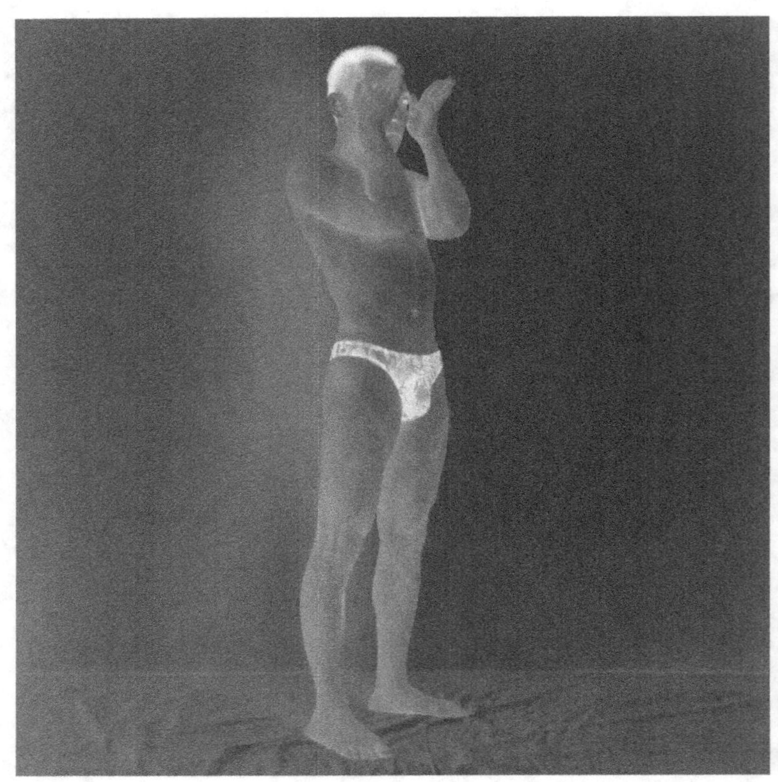

69

Killing sentences the meaning

Killing sentences the meaning of a gun,
even if you exaggerate my beauty
finally. Now I am worth worthless money.

Now I seemingly have anything but all,
still, you fail to analyse my charm, cause
desire adulterates the faith of a nun
despite a monk's heavenly hypocricy
of defending the intention of a gun.

God bless the blissful pregnancy of a nun
when/wherever truth pretends that crime serves law.

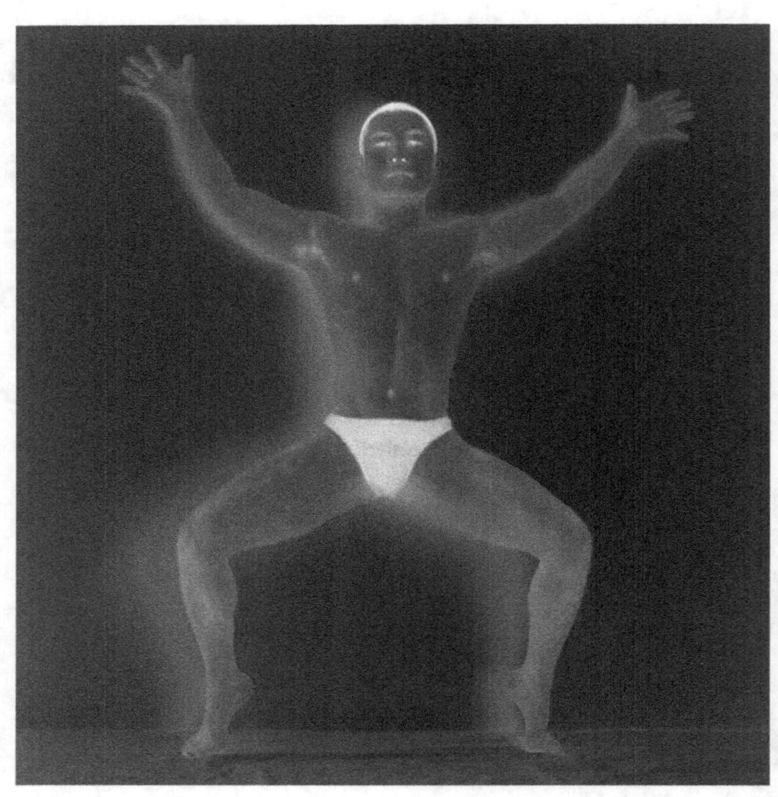

The Waste Land

To identify 10 bitches among
9 celebrities
            seems
                    quite seemly,
                            if

to verify 8 imposters among
7 artists sold out as ladies' man

requires
        less males
                but much more shemales than

to testify 6 deceivers among
5 politicians bought in by con men

who have killed
            to become
                    the fathers of
4 murderers among 3 policemen,

2 corpses among 1 not yet born man

or zero human in the waste land.

Nature is nature

74

Nature is nature whereas humans want
more food than hunger needs everything else,
the sky in the moon from yesteryear' spring,
for instance.

Human nature is nature
whereas animals are not the same kind,
there being not much difference between
a hunter and a huntee, if killing
must be a must.

Rainforests are nature,
deserts as well, with or without a tree
leaving a grass space to grow till sunset.

I am a misanthrope

I am a misanthrope

I am a misanthrope

I am a misanthrope making myself
in a world made by itself.

                    In a world
where questions (not all know the answers to)
outnumber answers (not all understand),
a misanthrope, being miserable,
stays hopeful for another world not made
but saved by itself.

                    However, a world
cannot be saved if it cannot be made
(unworthy of both miseries and hopes)
thanks to self-making misanthropes.

                              Ergo,
I remain a misanthrope till I die
in this world of neverending dying.

What makes a hero

What makes a hero
              makes better a coward
than whatever that doesn't make any sense
without trying to fail.
              Still, if a world
makes both heroes and cowards,
                          what more nonsense
does this world make without failing to try?

Perhaps
        the recurring histories of now
where everything recurs
                    without knowing why;
Never
        everyone's freedom to die, no.

My testament

I am as hell as the world near the end.
All I act are instints, all I know, fears
:
Limbs benumbed are stones blowing into sands;
hair on fire are trees burning into seas.

Skin feels bones, but bones feel no life;
flesh hurts soul, and despair gives up hope;
Lungs breathe until there is no time;
Blood runs until there is no road.

First I curse, soon pain remains fine.
Since early years truth has been told.
Surrender? Sure, still with a sigh.

Memories seem a dream ago
:
I allowed some bad when I wished much worse;
doing some good, I failed to play a god.
Judge me after you will fill in your hearse.
My testament shouts: "In this world I was born!"

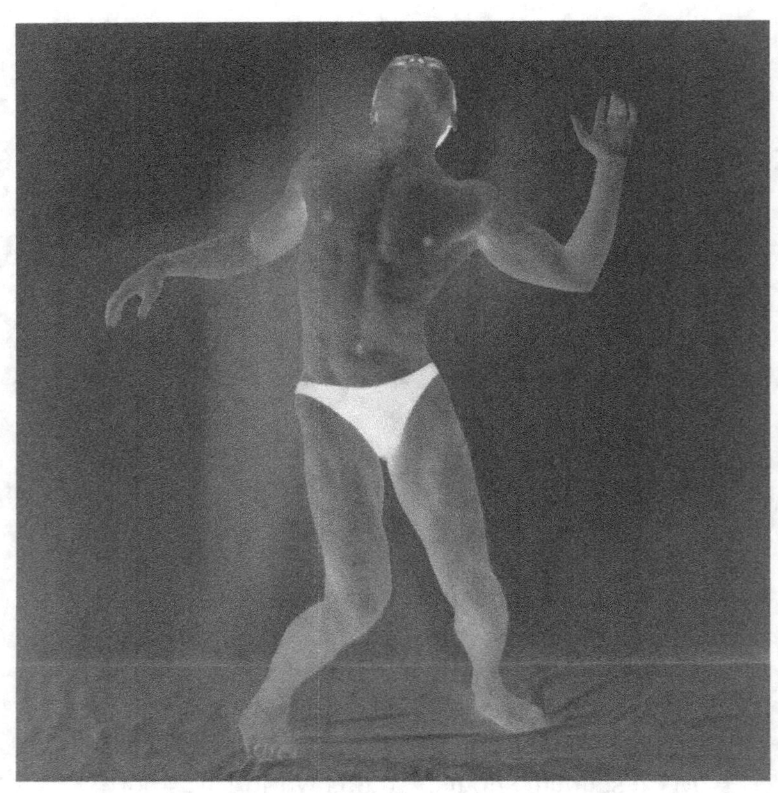

all too human

I am only human, all too human:
I devour my hunger before
my body decays;
I enrage my anger before
my hunger devours me;
I torture my pains before
my dreams deceive me;
I forget my dreams before
my anger enrages me;
I depreciate my body before
someone else disappoints me;
I sell my soul before
my life fails me;
I disappoint myself before
my soul is sold;
I fail my life before
my pains kill me.

Last and most,
I excuse my sins howbeit
my sins excuse me not.

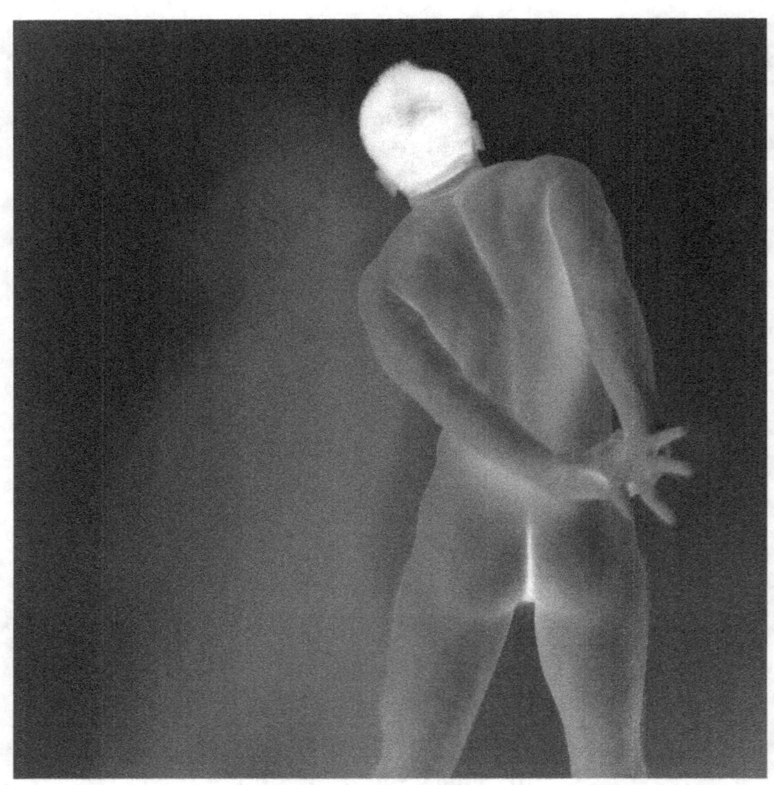

craziness is freedom at its most sane
celebrating the ultimate nonsense:
the law of the universe
that incarcerates the earth

life on other accidental planets
evolves outside of coincidences
even its states of mind are implanted
with knowledge defying subconsciousness

aliens are neutral like nonhumans
in their unnatural human nature

as an alien, I am free;
as a human, I am crazy

Selfishness

Selfishness confuses self-esteem with
itself.
    (Why wouldn't it if unselfishness
refuses to give more than everything?
Because everything taken is selfish.)

Selfishness does what unselfishness means
when self-esteem seems meaningless.
               (It doubts
the meaning of both seeming and doing
misunderstanding either is selfish.)

87

You have to become who you are

You have to become who you are

You have to become who you are
no matter who becomes someone else
under someanother else's skin.

Feel what your heart is made to feel
(better than you know all knowledge
(known to be useless
                              unless
no one feels more the same difference))
the only world
                    (firstly called life
as big as itself
                    as small as a sand).

Your becoming
                    is already your feeling
until your feeling is now
                              your becoming.

A ubiquitous sand

A ubiquitous sand

Let every chance compete with privilege
(privileged at every given chance
to choose among infinite planets),
the most privileged chance being
                              not to choose
(a ubiquitous sand on earth)
                        at all.

A ubiquitous sand on earth
is privileged enough to compete with
infinite planets (privileged enough
not to be chosen),
all chances being given only by the universe.

Where do all my emotions (dis)appear

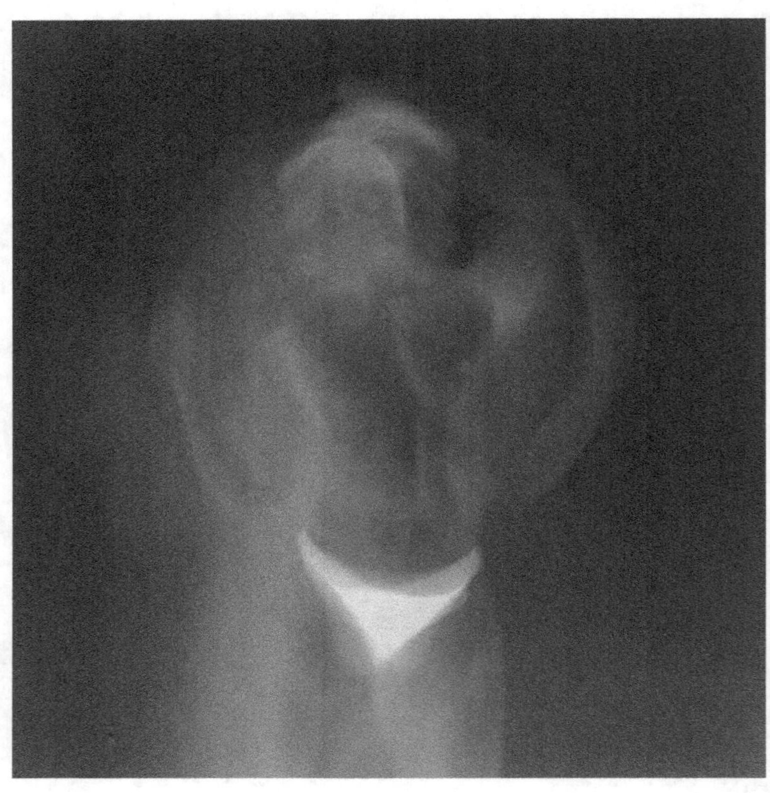

Where do all my emotions (dis)appear

Where do all my emotions (dis)appear
after feeling themselves the way I feel?
Partly somewhere I have (n)ever travelled,
wholly beyond any experience.

Wherever they find themselves,
                              love is there.
And love awaits until I (dis)appear.

For fear that hate should finely follow,
                                    we,
love & I,
          hide in our favorite place
where someone (un)familiar to life is
already.

          Life remains (un)familiar
to me with all my emotions feeling
the way death is born to feel more or less.

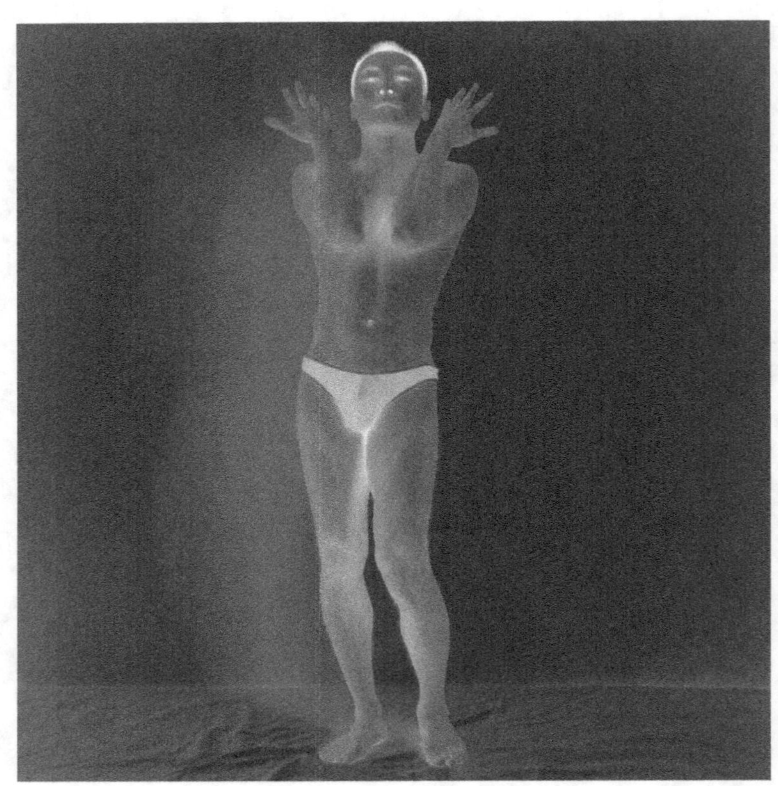

Growing somewhat old

Growing somewhat old is ever behind
feeling old enough all of a sudden.
I am somewhat young for myself before
I am young enough for my life and death.

Regardless, waiting is what I do best
from doings of beings which need a rest.
Evermore, loving is what I do worst
from beings of doings which I want most.

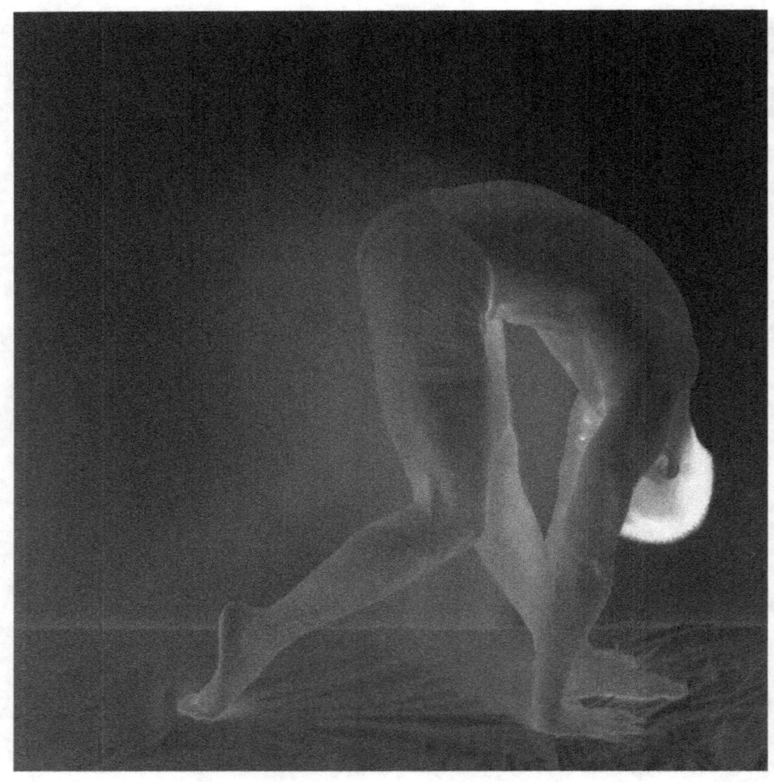

The loneliness of the earth

The loneliness of the earth grieves me
when I do not expect a soul mate
from outer space to understand me
(of the same chemicals we are made).

The lovelessness of the world hates me
when I am not being too worldly
like other members of my species
(for the same desires we choose to kill).

The hopelessness of life despairs me
when all life must learn the hopefulness.

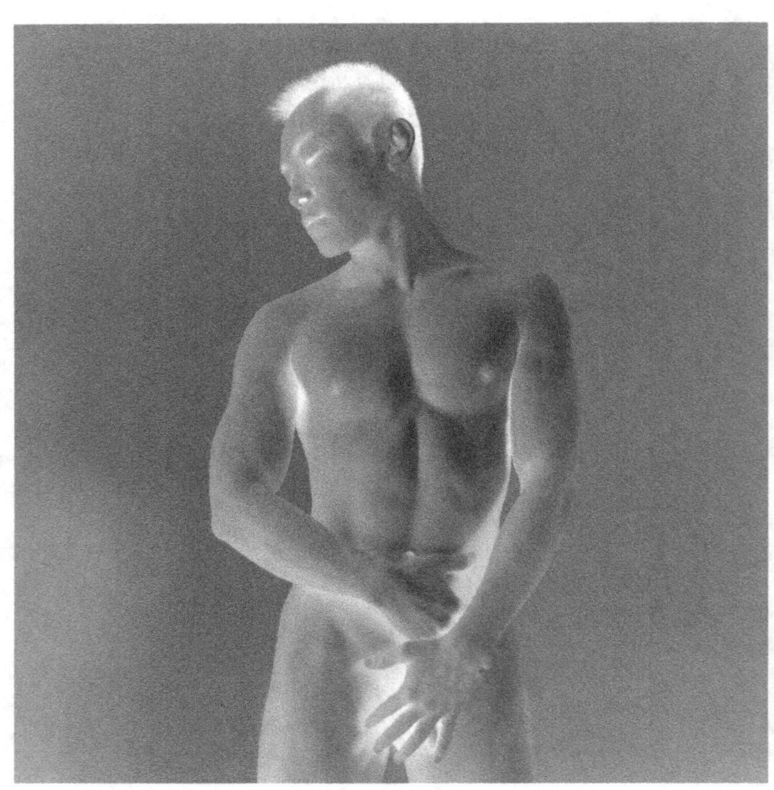

The history of grief

The history of grief
finds no beginning and loses no end.
Life and death have to be equally spent.
Good and bad mutually understand
that all beings happen on the waste land.

Time fulfills beauty in forgetfulness.
Even ugliness lives for its greatness.
Nothing but dreams are real in dreaminess.
Something is something else in consciousness.

Love loves hate if hate hates love in return.
Love hates love so hate loves hate, no return.
What is bigger than the biggest desire?
Answers the ice burning like freezing fire...

The history of grief
engraves everyone's grief of history.

Everything fades away

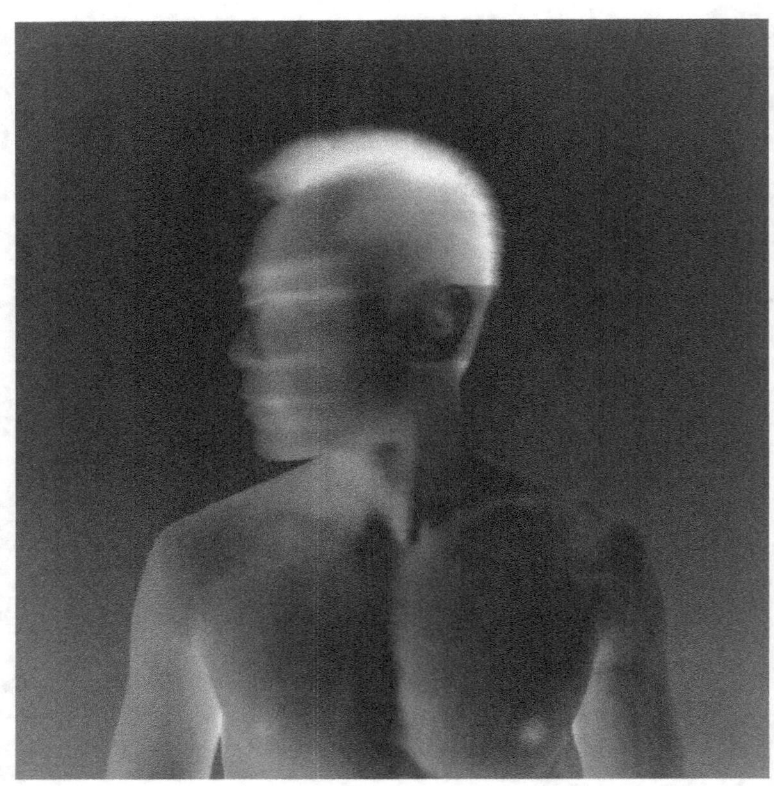

Everything fades away

everything fades away in its own way
as everything is made.
                    anyway,
everything lonely belongs to the same
family under different names.

everything happy forgets how to be
everything else temporarily.
still,
        everything remembers to be free
occasionally, till finally

something feels nothing that feels anything,
be it loneliness or happiness.

There

There

There, I shall live, where dreams come true,
no matter how false they must be.
There, love is abundant like trees,
leaves growing young in every breeze.

There, lives already somebody
that always appears in my dreams.
There, a life time equals a day
as long as a night around him.

There, a stranger is strange enough,
because friends stay close to nourish.
There, all families reunite
and death does in itself perish.

There, is not as far as heaven
but somewhere possible on earth.

REBIRTH

REBIRTH is a perfect human being
doing a forever imperfect world.

when comes here to make and goes there to mend.
where recalls another time now and then.
a dream is merely personal enough
to embody the person it dreams of.
truths belong to if, if forgets a lie.
between two extremes, all feelings feel fine.
love gives love as much as hate is taken
for granted as a reason mistaken.

REBIRTH is perfect yet we need to be
reborn in a forever perfect world.

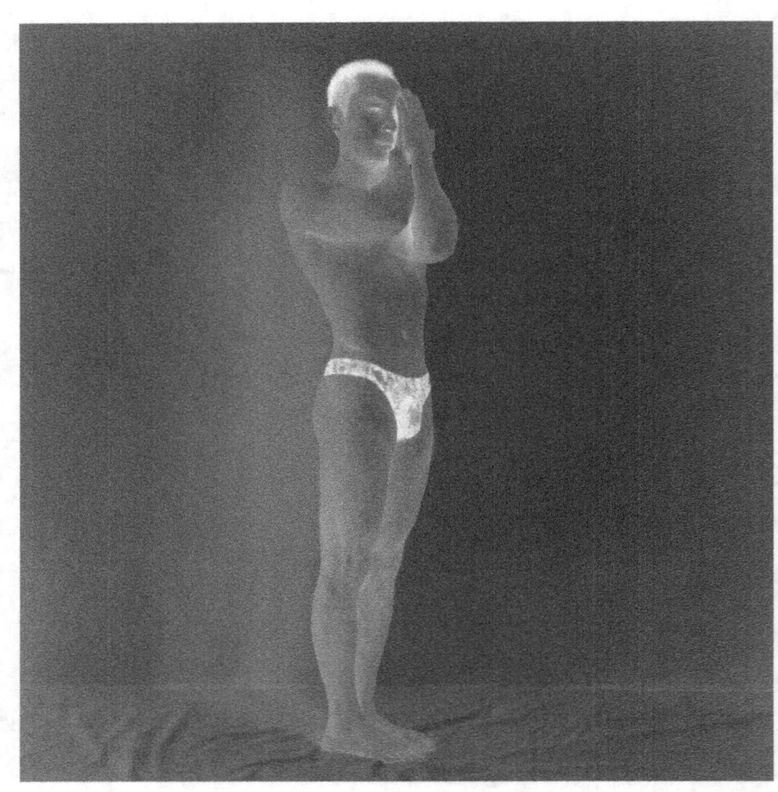

to be myself

to be myself

to be myself is impossibly
the opposite possibility to be
fair, but life is unfair,
                    unless (i am
as loved as why am i not the center
of the world?
                and the world is
as hated as everyone dreams the same
dream when no one sleeps)
i am merely someone else to someone
after all
            excuses have been used
and wasted with more reasons
making less sense.

the sooner i am myself,
the later i am not, until life is fair.

With every breath

With every breath in the blink of an eye,
I devour a piece of eternity,
greedily granting
                sex,
                        love
                                and beauty
that I cannot live without in my life.

When I am gready for
                        fame and fortune,
the moment of desire is satisfied
in every breath heavier than a sigh
answering(questioning)
                        all questions(answers)
                                        of existence.

everywhen life is enough

everywhen life is enough

everywhen life is enough
                    everywhere
the world forgets being a world
forgotten
          until
                  spring returns everyhow

remember
          love is enough

in rememberance everywhat is enough
dreamt between the world of outside
and inside a dream

everywhich season awakes a dream
from the world of both sides

love is spring in all seasons

yes is everywhy
                    i am everywho

memories, fantasies, realities

the disappearance of appearance grows
stronger than the impatience of patience.

memories memorise fantasies;
fantasies fantasise realities;
realities realise memories.

the knowledge of a lifetime fails to know
one depend on another's dependence.

a new circle reconnects all circles
lost between ascendence and descendence.

memories memorise fantasies;
fantasies fantasise realities;
realities realise memories.

null paradox in few paradoxes
happens to count from presence to absence.

Turn back one last time

Turn back one last time before you depart.
I stand where we both were, no longer are.
Your presence grows still stronger from afar.
Time measures the distance of worlds apart.

You were my dear sister and my dear friend
with whom I never had to learn to share.
I was every crushed dream that you could mend.
Between dreams and life, I see you again.

My tears made you sad, your pains hurt me, too.
One plus one compassionate more than two.
Above us, the colorless sky turned blue.
Without you, spring would not be colorful.

Henceforth, I must get accustomed to grief,
understanding that happiness is brief.
Somehow love is eternal, I believe.
Love is a tree upon which we are leaves.

No one mourns the person that you were not;
all accept your genuine right and wrong.
A miracle happened when you were born,
a miracle that will live on and on.

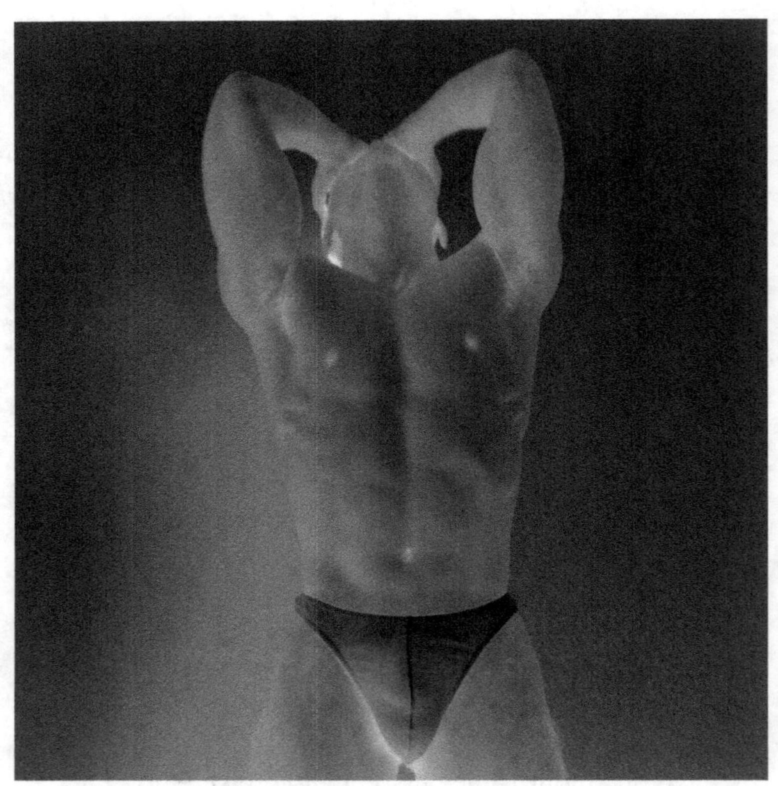

(un)fortunately

(un)fortunately, it happens a lot,
if it happens to me among many
who came to stay a while before leaving
from time to time,
place to place,
chance to choice.

if it shouldn't happen to me at all
from time to time,
place to place,
chance to choice,
i'd leave after i'd have come to stay a while.

(un)fortunately, i'm among many.

Once upon my death

Once upon my death

Once upon my death,
                    I determined
                                why
(because
            every life is predetermined)
I would never surrender to the world
(created out of hate)
                        succumbing to
enough love
            not loved enough by myself.

Once upon my birth,
                    I determined
                                why
(because
            miracles are predetermined)
I would ever surrender to myself
before enough love
                        loved enough by you
(created beyond the world)
                                loving me.

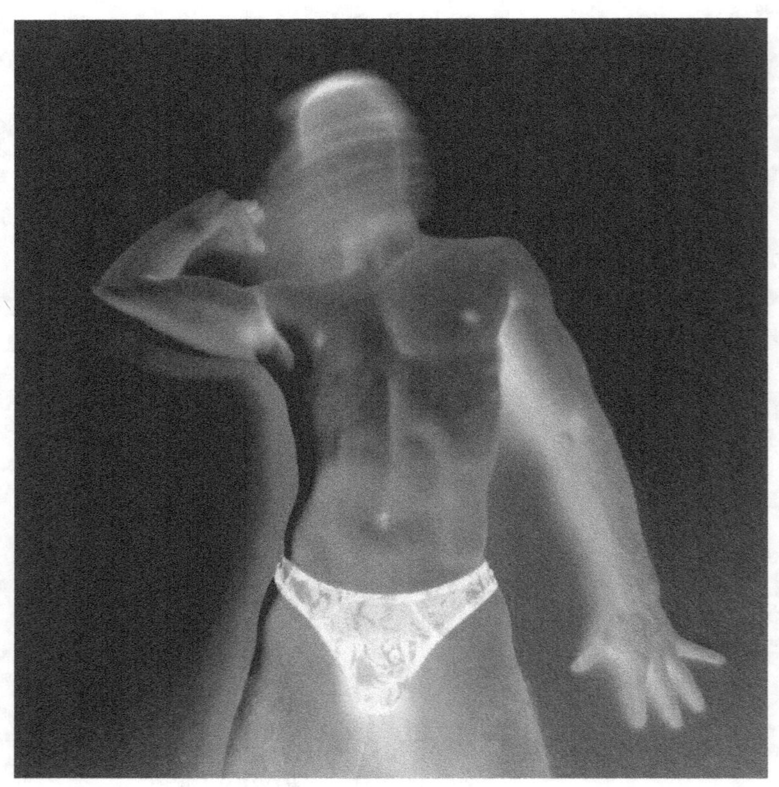

I regret everything

Because nothing is regrettable, I
regret everything.

                        I regret myself
including everyone trapped inside a
life, living a waking dream.

                              I regret
time, it changes more or less than it makes.

I regret war and peace with the excuse
of nature never needing an excuse.

I regret love whenever an imagination
wants to be real or a reality
wants to be anything but something else.

I regret death first and foremost lastly.

I regret life and death regrettably.

Art

Art is but a stubborn illusion
around a selfish disillusion
ment:
       all lies find all truths almost artless.

Eyes see eyes when colors are blind.
                         Aimless
sounds resonate with phenomenons.

Not every doom survives Babylon,
unless
       every craft rejects the basic
rule
   and
       every comedy feels tragic.

Anything is free to decide one beauty
or another
       in case something turns ugly;
nothing is forced to evolve in itself.

Smell logic out of emotions
               and help
science confuse a supernatural
myth.
     The universe grows universal
until we recall the cultured life
in the wilderness.
         Let's redeem art!

Beauty; Ugliness

Beauty is in the mind, only because
ugliness is already there and elsewhere.
Beauty is beautiful, only because
ugliness is ugly enough to be fair.

Beauty beautifies nothing but itself,
therefore,
it gives the entire human race no help.

Ugliness needs to remain as it is,
therefore,
it has the entire human race to please.

Isabella smiles

126

Isabella smiles bitter inside
the museum than sweet outside.

It's a holy different world inside
the museum than the same outside.

No one covets someone's favorite,
the original, stolen from Mona Lisa.

Among the crowd of paintings
anyone refuses to find Isabella.

Volcanoes in my house

Volcanoes in my house
                date back to stones
of consciousness
                and forth to dust in mind.

They erupt now&then changing calendars
and go extinct here&there changing atlas.

Thanks to them,
                my house has known the unknown
dangers;
                I have known the unknown knowledge.
Together,
                we make the world understand
the done being undone;
                        the undone, done.

All things coincide with all counterthings
granted that time&space grant encounters
(beyond time&space rules strangeness
beyond earthly intellection).

I am the sole existence in my house
where nothing exists except volcanoes.

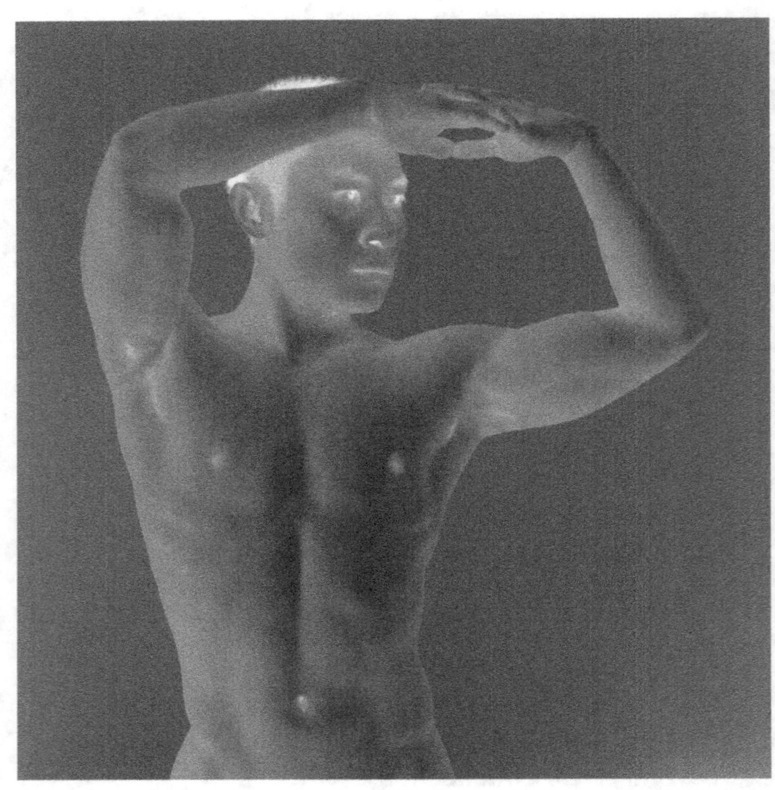

Procrastinate until NEVER

Procrastinate until NEVER is born,
time being neither somebody's nor mine.

Privileged
            (this unhappy manunkind)
to breathe in another next to last breath,
notwithstanding upon the corpse of death
(whose sealed fate of whose sin saving behind),
a self dreams no better than a night sleeps.

Inside the peace fight a million prisons;
outside a war, reasons excuse freedom.

Given meanings can be given to deeds;
taken nonsense makes sense in some senses.

Which is which,
                    either the worst or the best?
At least,
            a fool knows nothing dull;
                                at most,
history tastes as mondaine as burnt toast.

Dick, Percy & Annis

Dick, Percy & Annis find luck
at the butcher's wedding party
where flesh is flesh, bones are bones
and blood dares burst out of the veins.

Martha finds some luck, too, thanks to
Selena who makes everyone smooth
when s(he) mingles and tingles, all through
the endeavor of vigorous Tom.

Fincher & Hans only dream of
how Dick is born to find luck:
to be the bigness, hardness and wellness
inside of Martha, Percy & Annis.

The butcher may one day divorce,
but Dick, Percy & Annis will find luck
for the exultation of a Sperm Whale
nicknamed Moby Dick, Percy & Annis.

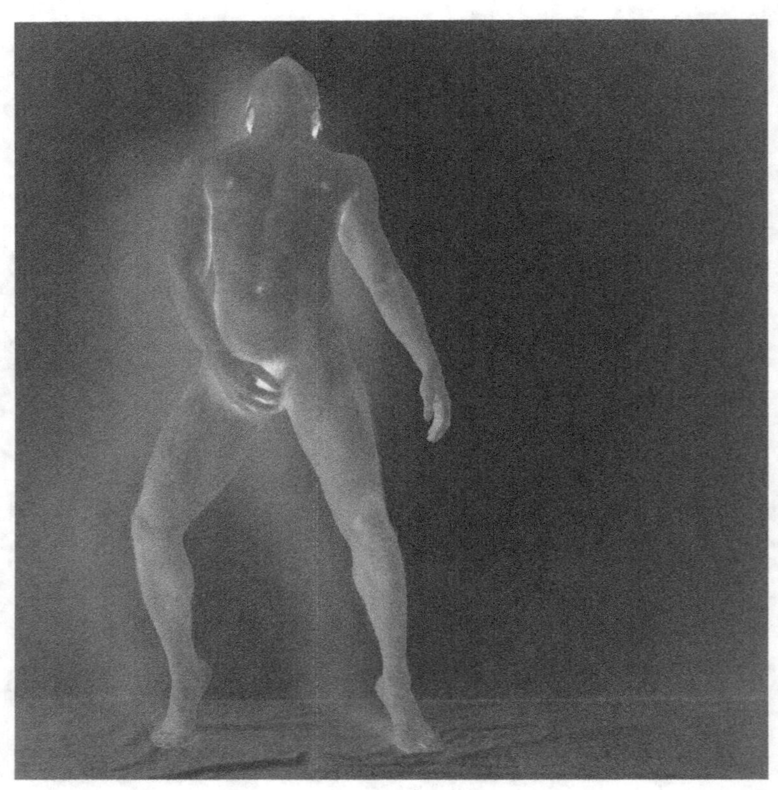

LIBIDO

LIBIDO LIDOBI BILIDO BIDOLI DOLIBI DOBILI

who's the next beast?
a bratwurst for breakfast.
the one the host lost in the east?
the pest a guest posted, whatever the cost.
is it easy to digest?
like a chest, a breast and a west waist.
did i hear a vast waste?
i meant the rusty ageist.
doesn't he need a rest in august?
we'll be all arrested in the moist forest.
including the past protagonist?
not if he takes a fist.
of the priest?
the prayer has nothing against it, at least.
does the utmost atheist protest?
guess who must molest a rapist.
can i just suggest...?
then i just detest...
the incest between a feminist and a sexist?
not of my slightest interest.
in contrast to your thirst for a communist?
lest i should be blasted with robust disgust.
isn't that a fast outburst?
in German, fast is almost.
are we in the midst of a jest?
you're not a humorist.
how about some trust?
either the best or worst, but not the last.
will the lust restart from the first?
nur wenn du fickst.

Drunk

135

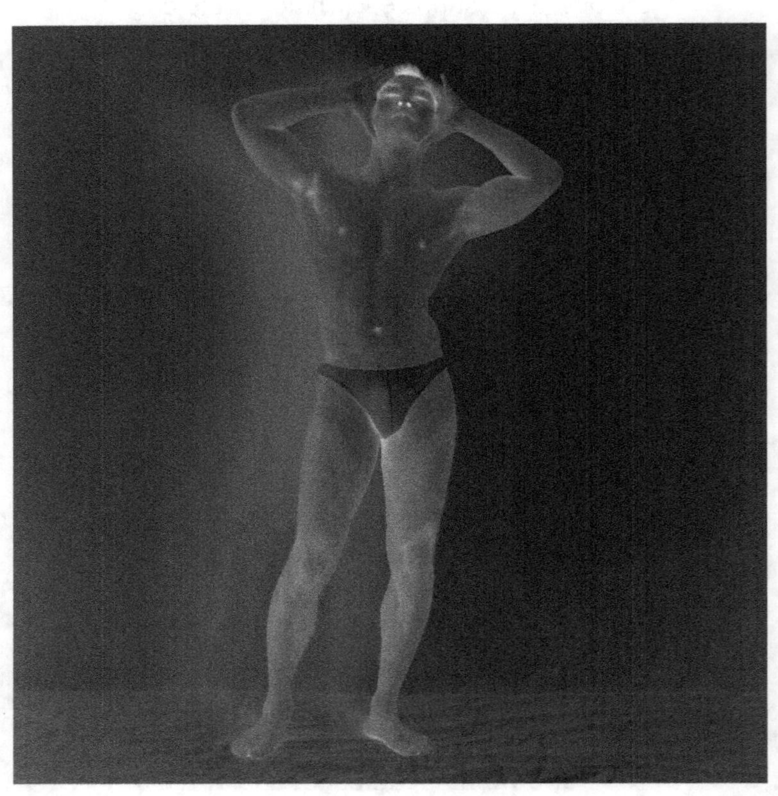

Drunk

As I am not drunk enough yet,

november blowjobs december
ready to be fucked by next year
(days seem more day and feel no pain;
nights seem more night and feel the same).

Every year fucks its twelve months.
All years are drunk enough to count
the same amount of pains in life
(life is just life in every life).

Funny how people look forward
(whether being drunk enough or
simply drinking to get drunk soon)
but no one sees the final doom.

I am timely drunk enough now.

STAR

STAR glitters beyond bastards
born out of true love a love much true
should the sex last long and longer
than an audience to rid a book
above a reel role model
her skin gets unrolled at faschist shows
there spiritual symbols
as so n so becum sexual
in the name of art n fart
on the pursuit of heaven n hell
promised by fame n fortune
they make this world chase after the tail
on the face of yes a star

if the wide-eyed audience could dance
in their narrow minds minding
no life of their own
                    give them a chance

Luck is the magic

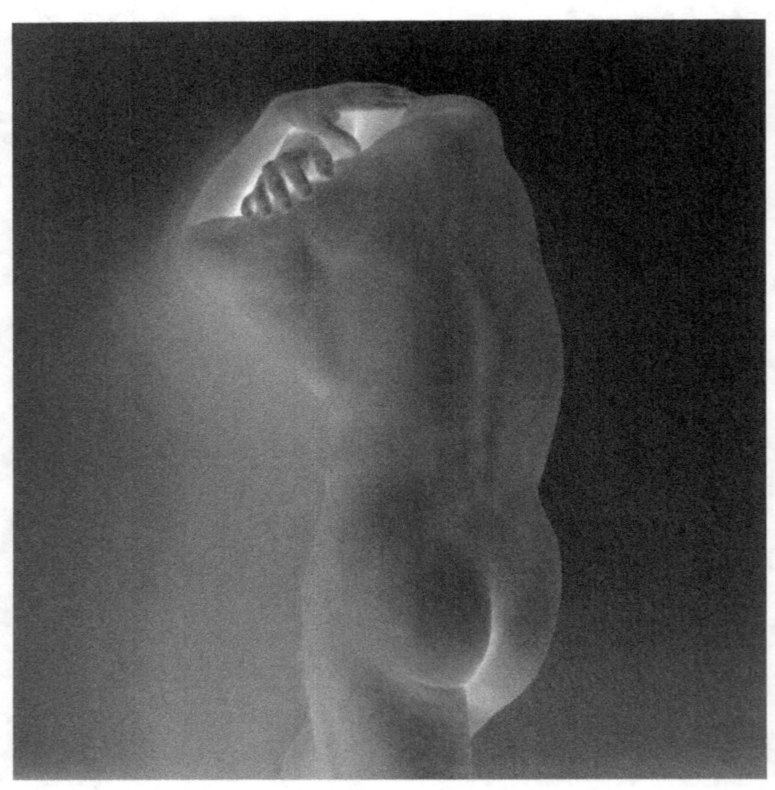

Luck is the magic of life if life is
magical
            at all.

                What else am I dismiss
ing to excuse life?

                    Excuse me, a lot.

But life is inexcusable, unless
all thoughts are wise, all words are equal
and all actions simply react to life.

Life is magical merely due to luck.

Still, luck is the magic. Luck is (un)real.

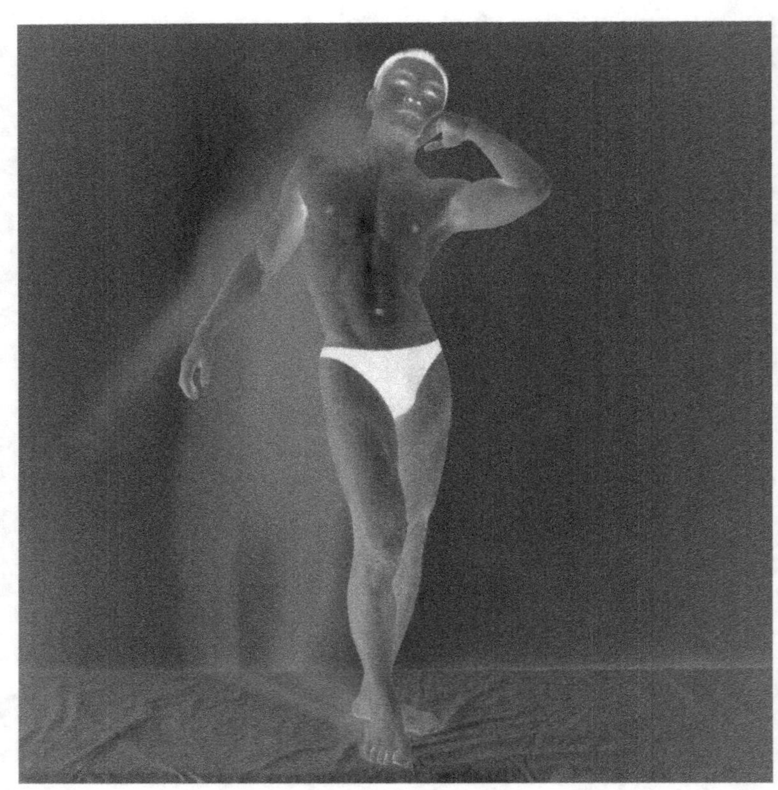

142

I wish
(not even pray)
somewhere in time
&
someday in place,
someone would die
somehow
from his or her unrequited love for me.

Much importance
would recall
much insignificance,
my own death, for instance.

Jealousy

Had jealousy feelings, it should be feeling me
(craving you only).
                        I am surely not wise
since I will not make sense. But I am
full of doubts beyond anger which is
discovering other emotions while
the world is collapsing inside of me
(outside is built with ruins)
                                    and noises
are crying. How do I must stop thinking?

Jealousy is a killer and it is killing me
till I am already (as) dead (as alive
still).
        Lastly, I am falling asleep, cursing
the impossible,
                    when they belong to
you and me in my dreams.

Jealousy is (becoming me for) me.

Hurt others

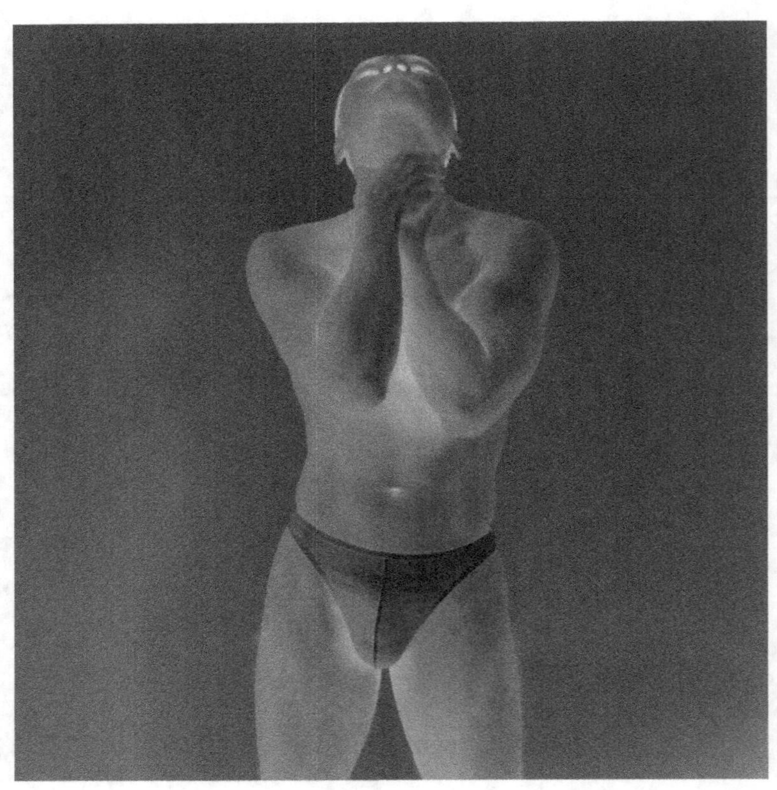

Hurt others

Hurt others
(who are hurt by your thoughts, words and actions of duty)
who
hurt me first
(inducing enough of hopelessness in humanity)
everytime
I hurt you
not as a consequence of my surrender to reality,
but as a paradox that
I love you.

...what a pity.

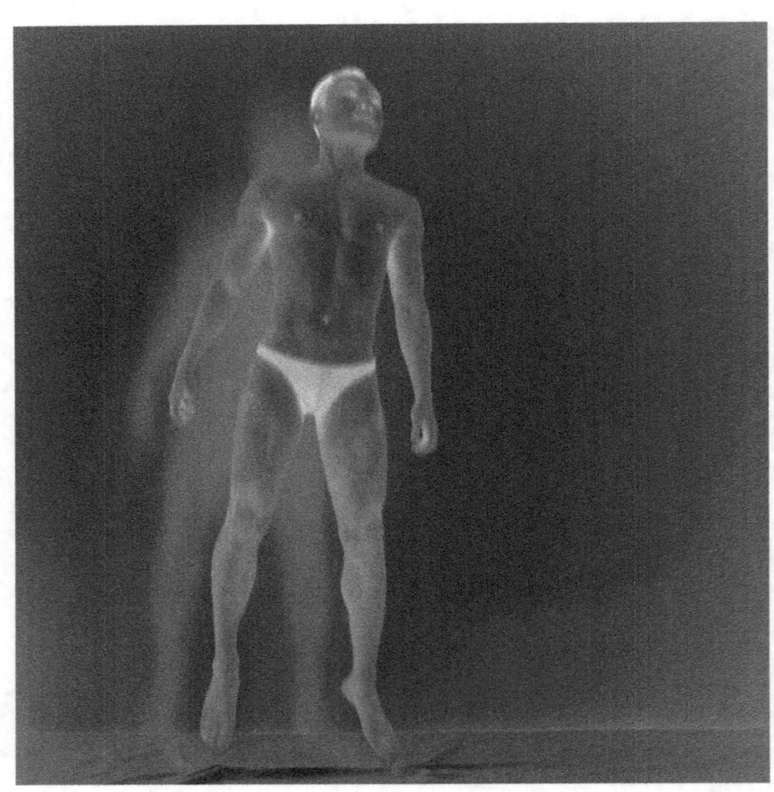

All bubbles continue to grow

All bubbles continue to grow
                         (And
tiny people in the bubbles
continue to be whoever they never are)
until
all worlds end, not with bangs, but whimpers.

Until this world (Where
both of us are personally someone else
floating like everyone else in the bubbles)
ends,
neither of us love (until either of us can)
life as a possible accident
(unconditionally,
death is an accidental possibility).

Our being together, however, stays
emotionless towards ourselves.

i want you infrequently

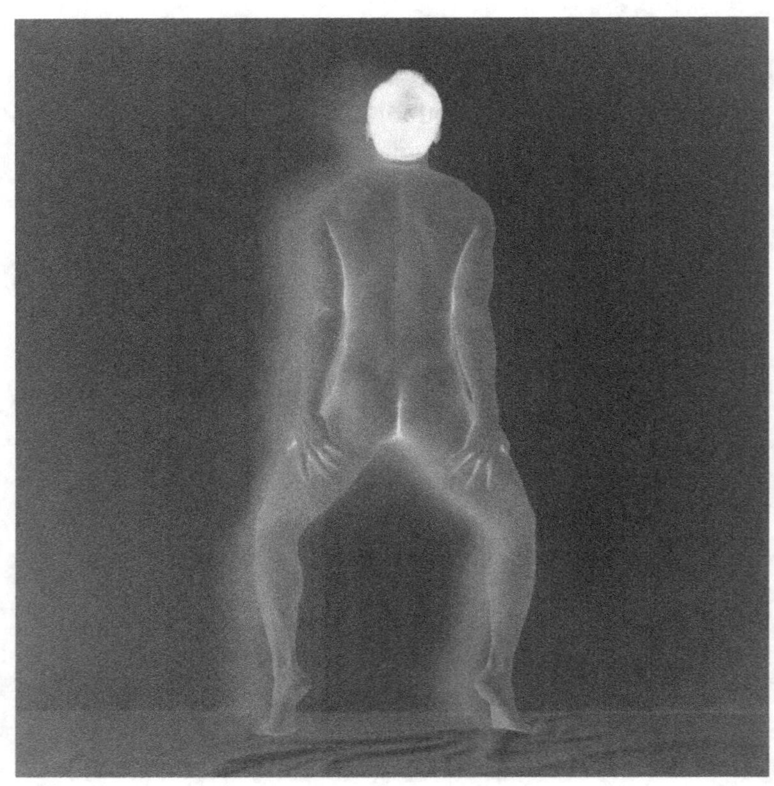

i want you infrequently

149

i want you infrequently

i want you infrequently less and less
at that next unhappening lips to lips
i defend my fake promise yes O yes
for nothing between us is love but sex

i miss you infrequently less and less
after this now happening face to face
i offend my true promise yes O yes
for one thing beyond us is love in sex

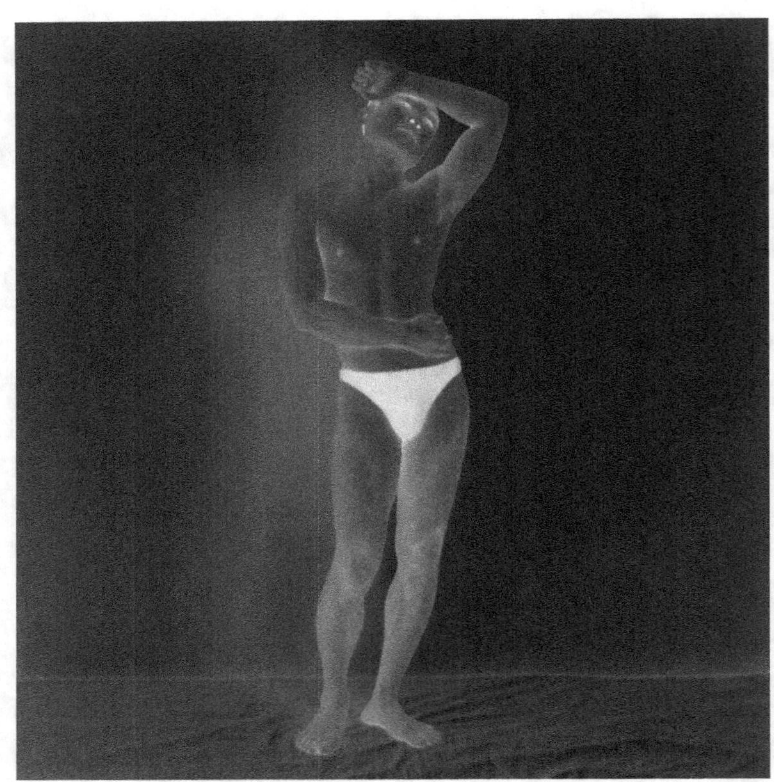

Simply difficult is love

Simply difficult is love
                    (when
I must be loved before you
love me
          already more than truly,
true is how a word means
you must be loved)
                    to understand why
(love is
          either early or late
between the two in love
(either this or that,
                    either I or you,
either either or or))
because
          love is (until love is not)
simply
          a word
                    difficult
                              to do.

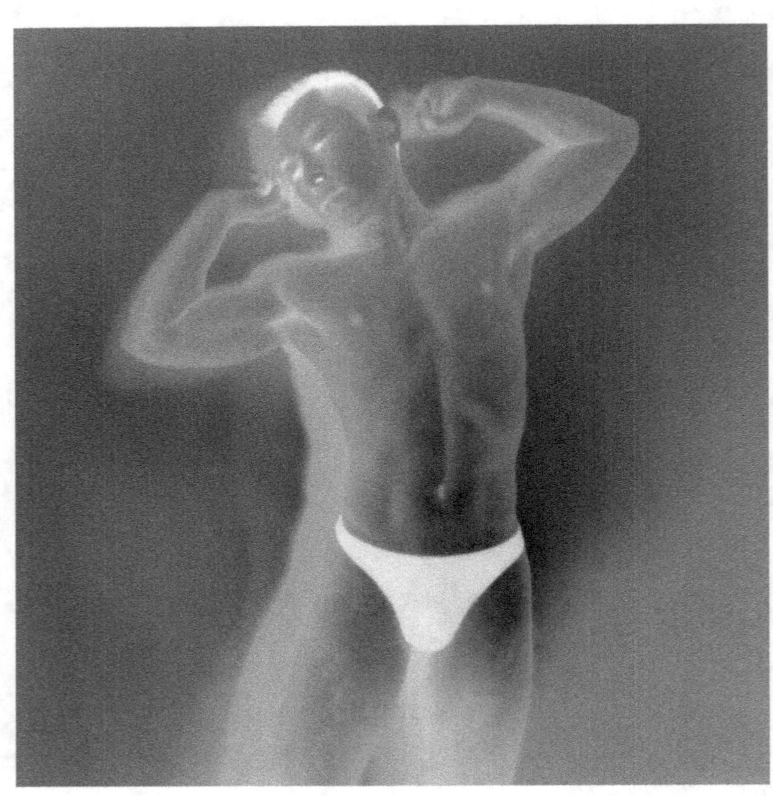

Having been awake all day

Having been awake all day,
                              I'm afraid
I'll be (as) sleepy (as my loneliness)
for the rest of my life.
Wasted is my whole life
failing to stay awake.
Wasted are days falling asleep
when nights pass by,
when love passes by till I die.

Having been asleep all night,
                              I'm afraid
I'll be (as) awake (as my loneliness)
for the rest of my life.
Wasted is my whole life
failing to fall asleep.
Wasted are nights staying awake
when days pass by,
when love passes by till I die.

Time is still hesitating before all
(bodies refusing to carry spirits,
passions being too shy to paint a brush
and winds seeming indifferent to breaths)

at this moment when
our distance is in our nearness.

I am happily sad
to confess
:
I am sadly happy.

Both wasted,
neither is the one for the other.

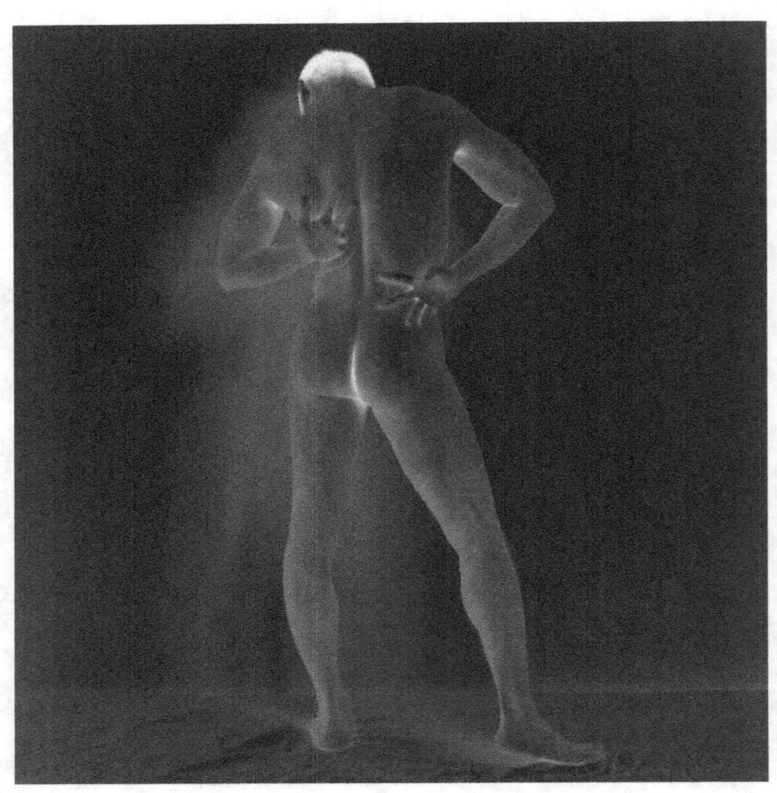

To love and to be loved

To love and to be loved
could not be
both in the time of changing seasons,

when one
pines for last year's snow
and the other
repines for next year's rain.

But you and I
could be,

until
forever 's sun meets never's moon.

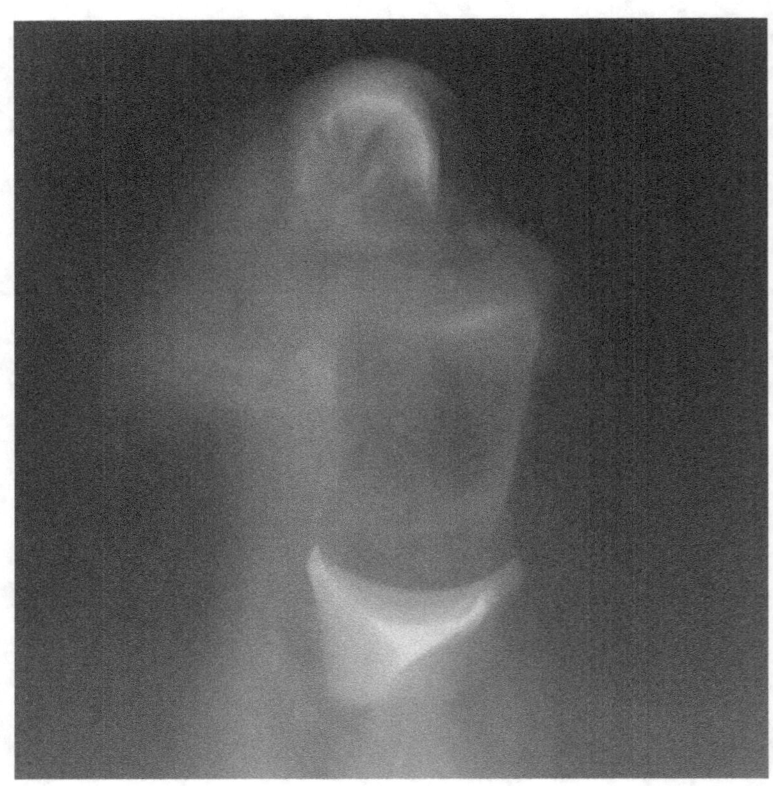

Love without lovers

Love without lovers
finding home in a heart,
all hearts
lose themselves among
lovers without love.

It is not a lost and found dilemma,
but an accident
between everyone and everyone else.

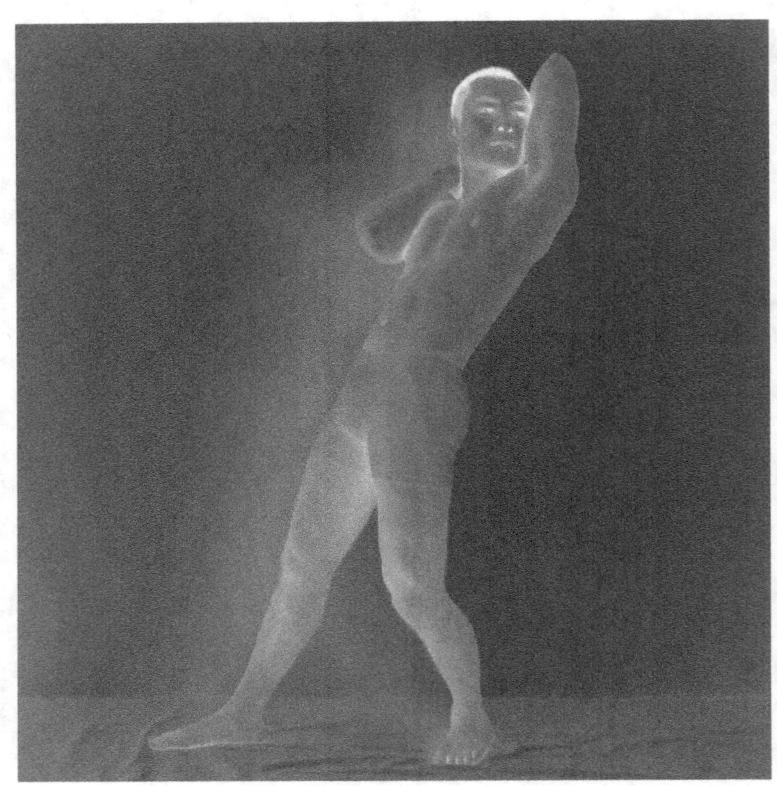

Among my many basic needs

Among my many basic needs,
your body comes before all o
ther delicious flesh within reach.

Hungrily, I won't miss any
flesh at any given chance. Your
body makes me call you daddy.

Your body beats my craving for
love, the tasteless love in my mouth.
Love's a craving, and that's all.

Body to body is enough
if soul to soul tastes platonic.
You and I are just animals.

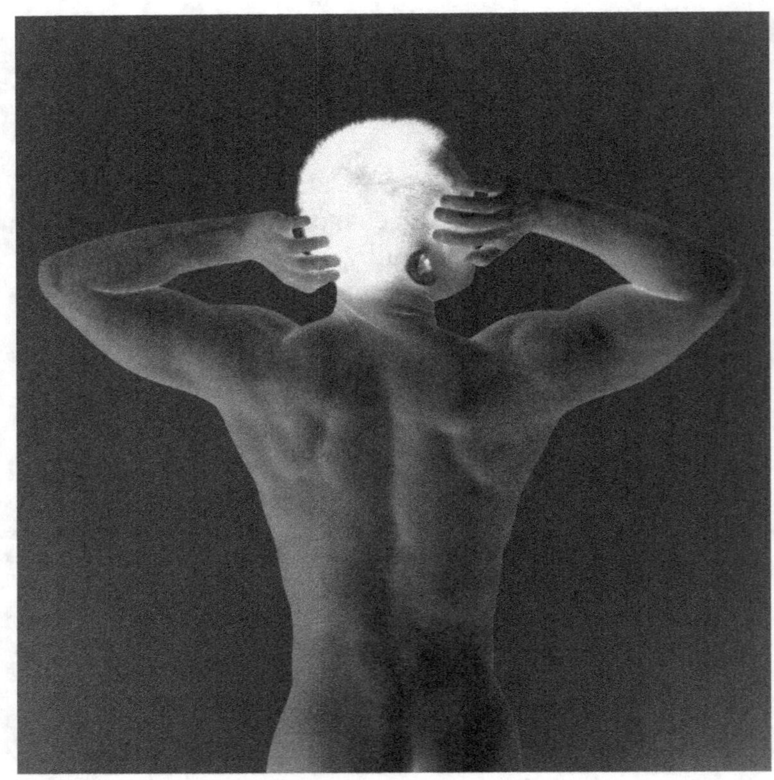

Sex is honestly the most honest

Sex is honestly the most honest
                              when
honesty desires hunger no less than
thirst,
        dishonesty fearing something else.

The conflict with no winner is endless.

In case honesty and dishonesty
envy agreement and disagreement,
marriage and divorce ask to remain free
after both sides have received the payment.

Each right is wrong
                    until each wrong is right.
Sex is honestly either right or wrong.

Each wrong seems right
                        because each right seems wrong.
Love is dishonestly not wrong but right.

my beauty envies my sexiness
once in a while,
                    twice on a roll
whenever my confidence determines
whatever my incompetance deceives

i am as beautiful as
                    (i kiss to kiss
a mirror only shy of a voice
confessing:
i am as sexy as)
                    self

Sexually depressed Tchaikovsky

Sexually depressed Tchaikovsky,

do I dare to understand you?
do I not want
                (need) to be you?
do I,
     did I,
            will I hear my
self sexually depressed in you,
as the notes kissed then
                          departed,
as the melodies fucked and
                           sucked,
as the love unspoken but
                          died?

Sexually depressed genius,
                          you
were depressively musical.

ugly people

When two ugly people are inlove,
I don't under stand,
They mustbe acting.

Or,
I mustbe super (face)ially re acting.

My pretty one,
You tell me,
Whether being inlove is under stan(double),

Or,
super (face)ial?

no one is proud of me

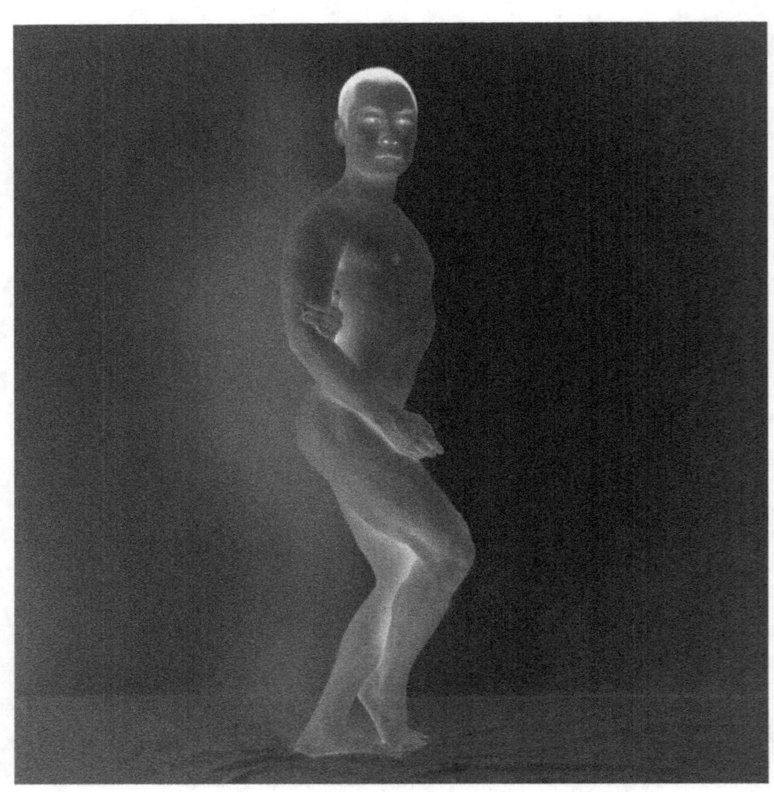

no one is proud of me

The shame that
            no one is proud of me
(more than I am less proud of someone
who wins and fails
                outside of my world)
is
my last but first pride that
                    humbles me
(as much as the middle envies none
who live and die
                inside their own world).

Nothing would rather be

173

Nothing would rather be

Nothing would rather be the last hope
if everything was worldly to know
in another humanly owned world
with animals baring human souls.

However, humans are animals
wherever nature wins as a whole.

Automatically, let machines run
out of flesh, blood and bones for fun.

What wants to be done needs to be done;
what has come will be gone, but for once.

175

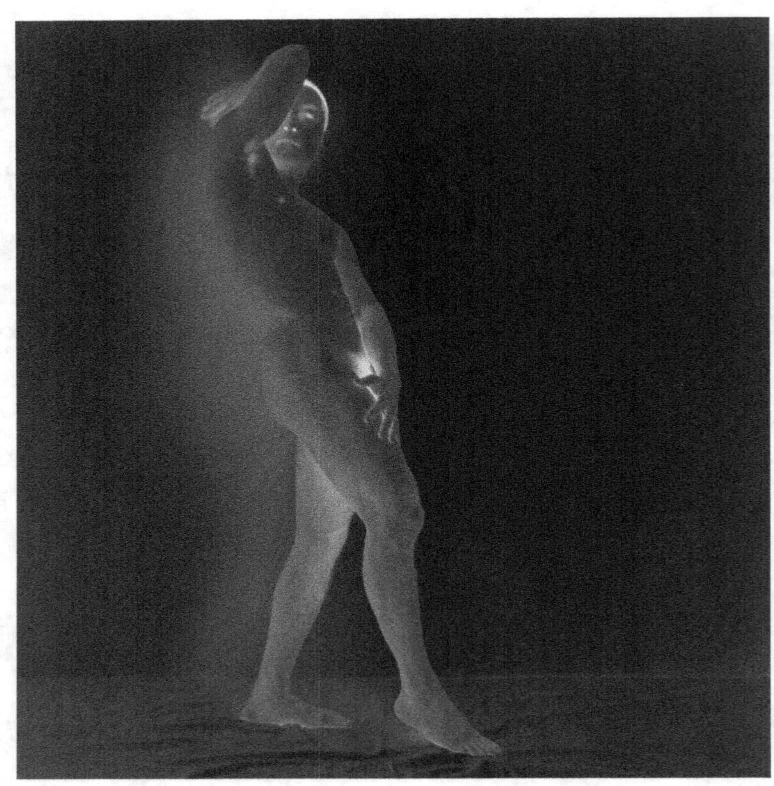

Even boredom is bored

Even boredom is bored

Even boredom is bored among boring
people. While some actions are finding reasons,
others are losing reactions instead.

Actions bore to be bored by reactions;
people bore to be bored once and for all.

What a crime it is to be born to be
boring! Such a crime must not be redeemed
from the failure of a single genius,
because boredom wins at the mercy of
survival which enjoys anything but
boredom.

So everytime the world cancels
life, survival becomes enjoyable.

And everytime the world seems livable,
boring people are bored of more boredom.

the rock of rocks

the rock of rocks am I rolling up
Sisyphos by and by rolling down.
the rock of rocks am I rolling down
Sisyphos by and by rolling up.

my weight lives the immortality
killing the weightless mortality.
my heart throbs the heart of punishment
whose length consists of my each moment.

human as I am, I do not do,
though being very much to be done.
after I am done, I still undo
the new oldness yet to be undone.

the rock of rocks am I rolling up
and down and down and up Sisyphos.

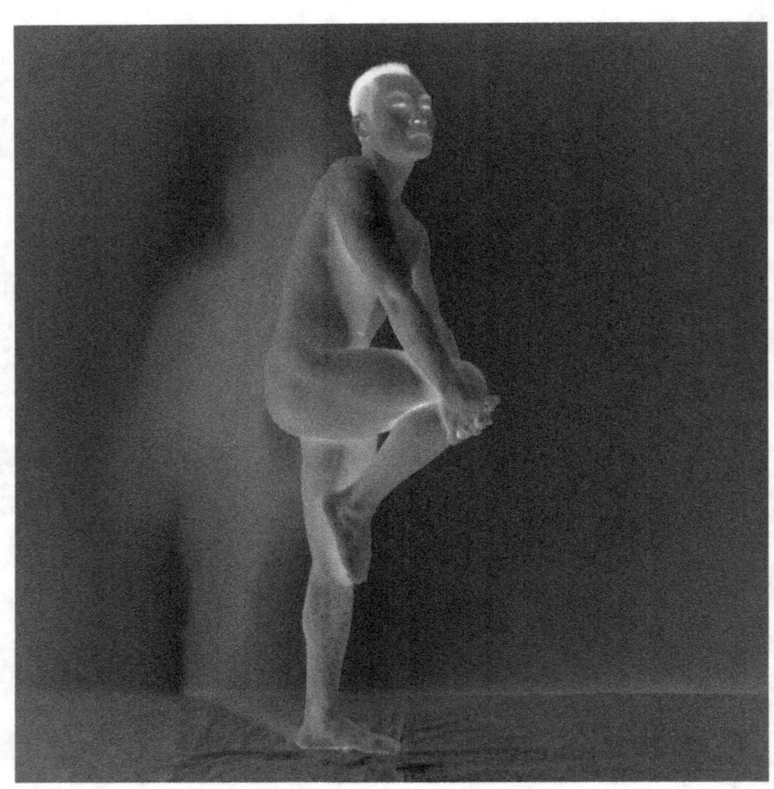

Idiocy

Idiocy deserves a full triumph
over the last drop of humanity
forasmuch as blood and sweat must be shed.

Hence, idiot, undo all your smartness
with all your smartness and other goodness
which mother nature did not give birth to.

Speaking of mother nature who is fucked
by her most motherfucking children, yes,
she is innocently responsible
if a mouth is not merely made to eat.

And a brain is not merely made to think,
but, moreover, not to think. Jesus Christ!

Diogenes the dog

Diogenes in thy old genius
asks why to answer because,
                              and he finds
a man to a man is no difference;
a slave and a king excuse all humans.

Did he not doubt the will of a finish,
he might persuade the dead to hang alive.

Less is enough
                when
                         more diminishes.
But the sun is fundamental,
                              Alex.
The greatest
            is to live the greatest
pleasure of a simple moment like this.

A dog is a god,
                whatever the case
may be,
        after the bones have gone to waste.

Knowing oneself is one's business only,
lest water should also wish to be drowned.

Come hell or heaven,
                         he sits on the ground,
knowing too much about philosophy.

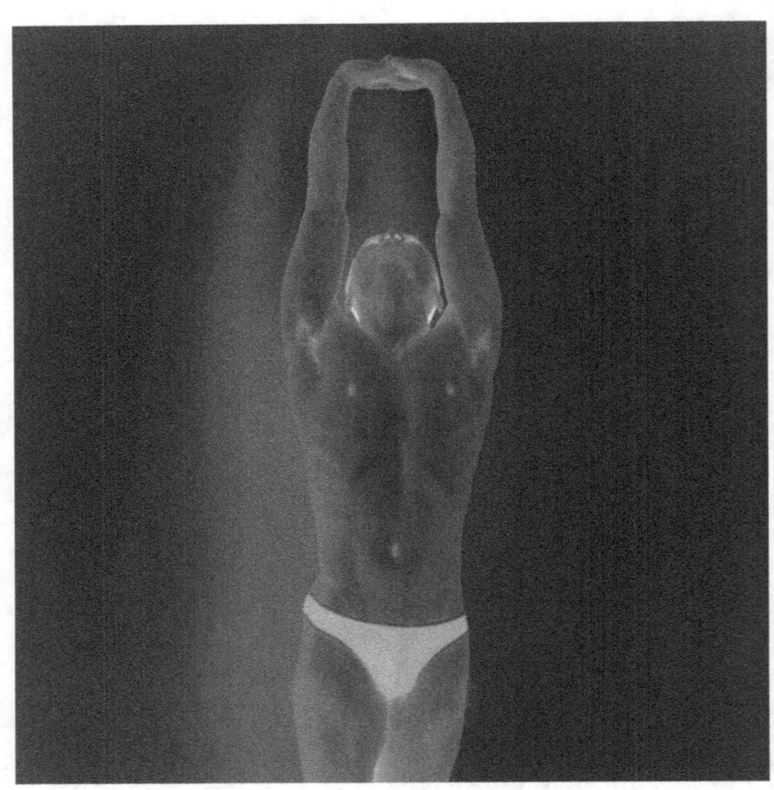

A king or a queen

A king or a queen is every body
being human among other bodies.

Socialising kills a better version
of hunting with no blood had to be shed
(slyly for animals,
                          hunger knows when
to stop).
              Another nature's creation
that destroys its last exemption.
                                        (Punished
are kings and queens by their supreme power
over kings and queens who are still childish.)

Sometimes, justice fairly serves crime somewhere
(a place where kings and queens embrace).
                                        Although
the road to hell is paved with intentions,
heaven never reveals the direction
and the whole world has to go high and low
to locate the deepest hole.
                          Continue
digging until apocalypse sees through.

185

Light speed travels through life spans

Light speed travels through life spans
whereof
eternity is the universe
away.

In the dimensions of humanity,
someone's ascendants compute
no one's aliens
                    somewhere;
sometime
            someone's aliens
regret no one's descendants.

By the laws of inhumanity,
e
   v
      e
         r
          y
            dwarf turns
black,
       white
            or red
worming into a black hole.

Burn out the evolucivilcolonization,
should
absolutely relative theories value on earth.

187

One equals two

One equals two in a world where fire
is a solid, a liquid and a gas.
Two envies three in this world where ice
agrees with everything fire is against.
Three mistreats four, five misuses six,
and seven misunderstands eight
enough for fire to freeze when ice heats
nine cold nights into ten hot days.

Fire or ice, either will suffice
within numbers of pure desires.

What important is somewhere I belong
for what important is the things unknown.
What more important is to look closer
as far as all importance disappears.

What the most important is the last hope:
to divide infinity by zero.

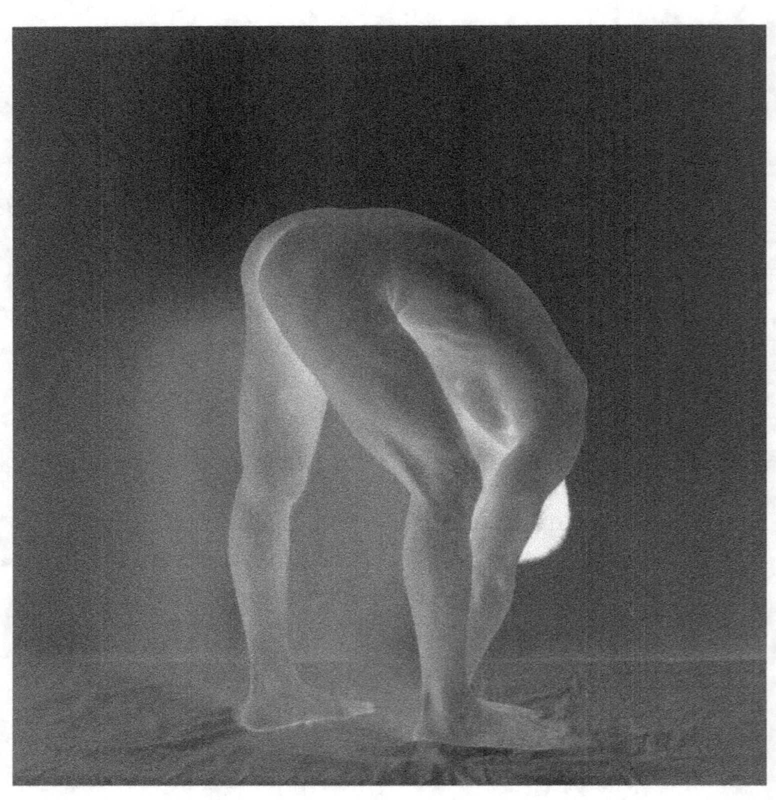

truth

there is one truth (above all truths)
that does not concern life or death
that lasts more than a million years
that outspaces the universe

there is no truth (below all truths)

my life could end

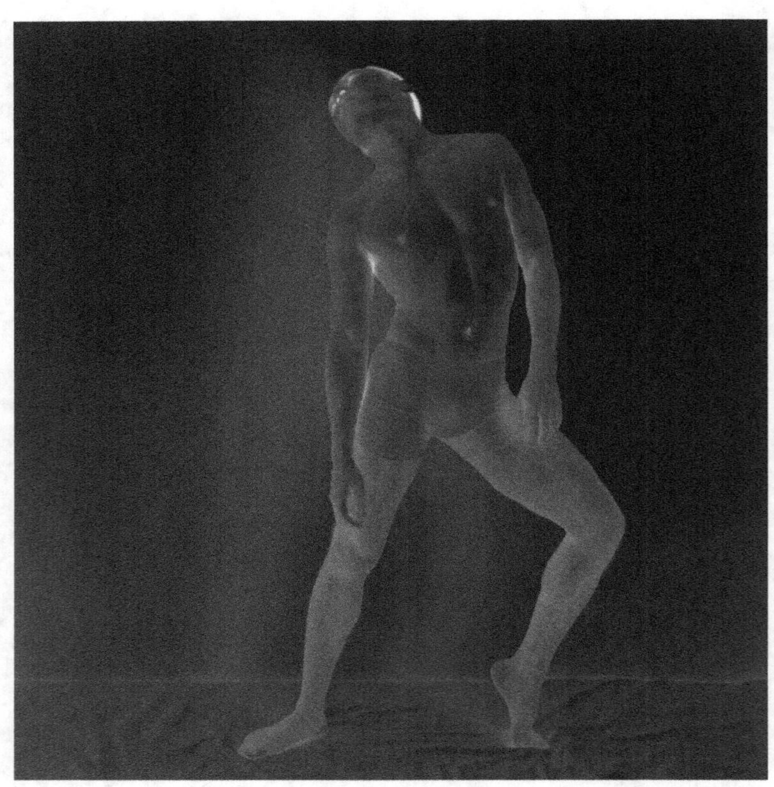

my life could end

my life could end at any moment,
however,
          my life should not end
at this moment
                    where
i write to be misunderstood,
                              or
at the next moment
                        where
i take this one for granted,
                              or
at the moment after
                        where
i regret wasting all the moments before.

my death prognosticating my life,
my life would end at some moment.

Rest In Peace

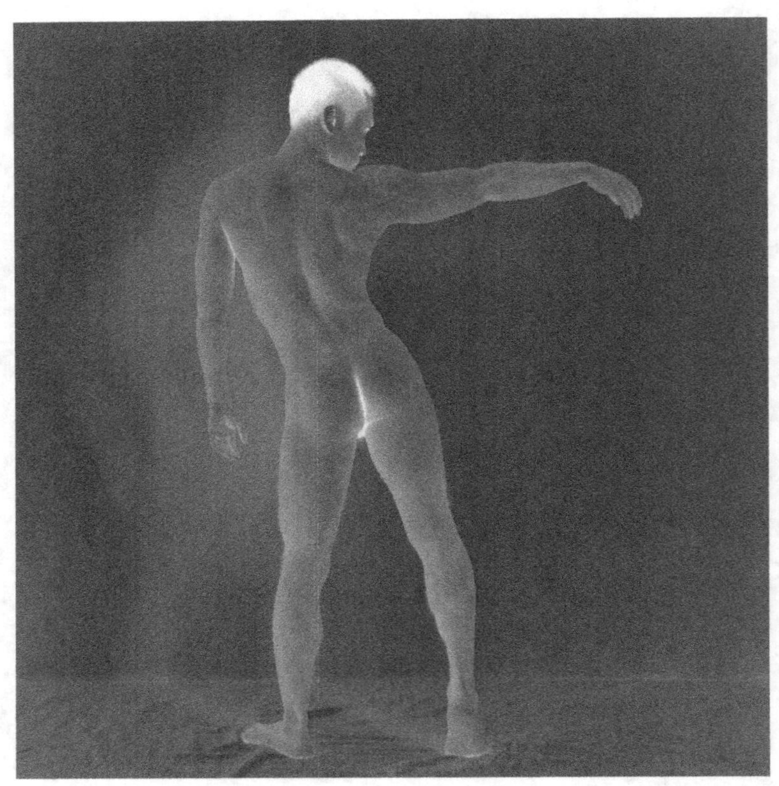

Rest In Peace

Rest In Peace to all that never happen
unless time and space measure each other.

The only chance before another loss
finds
two brand new eyes seen by twice déja vu
of
one hundred no telling one thousand yes.

Thus,
Rest In Wars to none of that happen, too.

To all that must happen out of logic:
the will to believe the truth of magic,
enough memories in oblivion
and an idiot in a genius
that resides deeper in an idiot,

Rest In Whatever the world may offer.

wanting PLUS knowing EQUALS giving

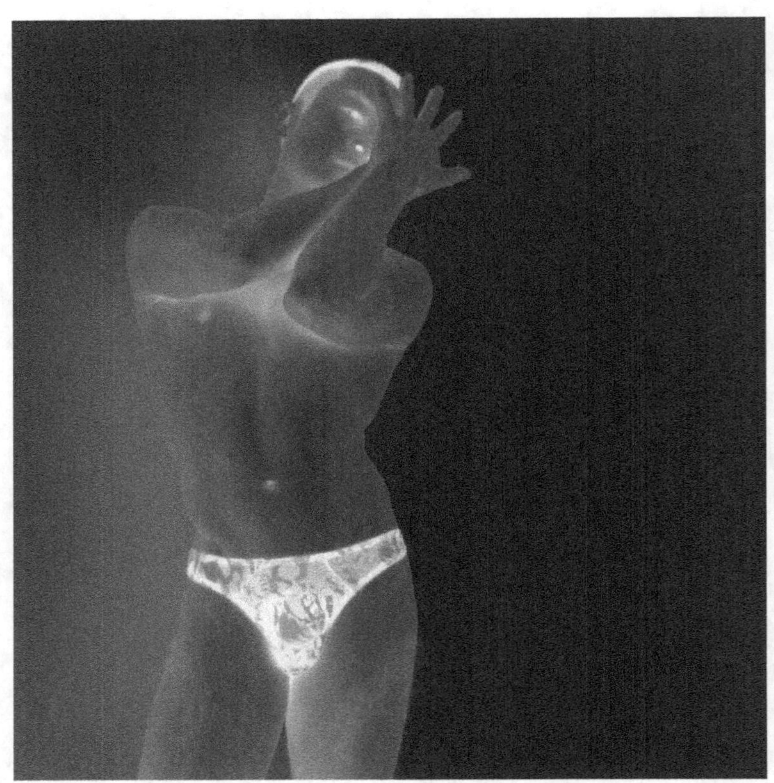

195

wanting love wholly than sleeping alone
partly in one's almost waking life
                              PLUS
knowing love selflessly than fearing death
naturally as long as nothing lasts
EQUALS
            giving love firstly to others
(both wanting and knowing love certainly),
next to the unhumanly doing things
(neither wanting nor knowing love simply).

The roads not taken

The roads not taken make no difference
for I have miles to go before I sleep
(not before I return to innocence).
I count every mile on the road beneath,
till the boundless sky meets the endless sea.

The sky and the sea are one song for me
as long as the years measure my heartbeat
(as long as the roads make no difference).
I still have years to sleep before I dream
and finally return to innocence.

granted

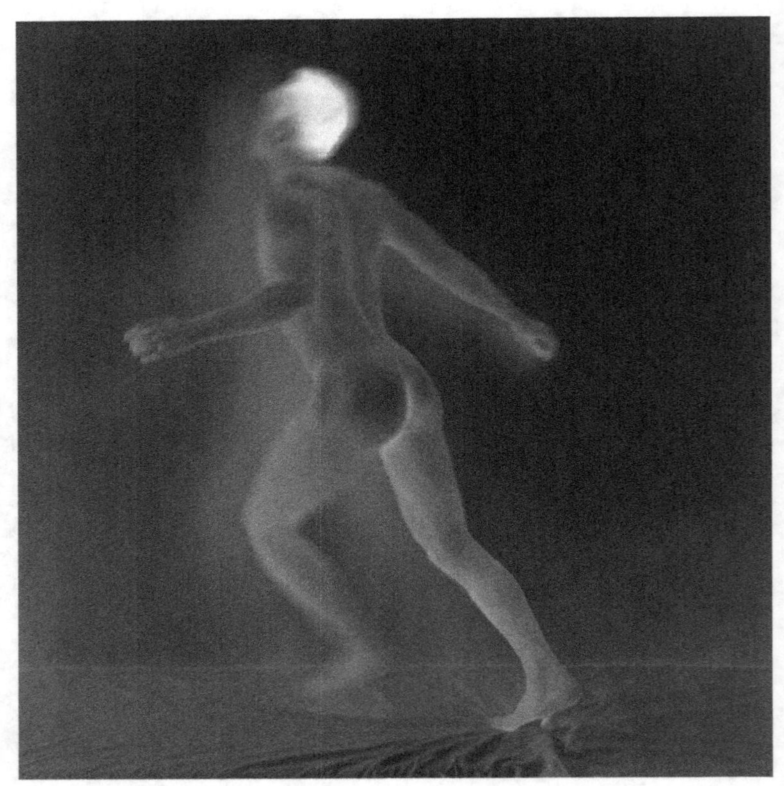

granted, now dreams to forget forever
but forever sleeps to remember now.
whichever nonsense time has to avow,
then wakes to eventualise never.

granted, here runs to satisfy somewhere
but somewhere walks to dissatisfy here.
whichever nonsense space has to endear,
there stops to substantialise nowhere.

INDEX OF TITLES